THE DYNAMICS OF GENERATIVE CHANGE

GERVASE R. BUSHE PH.D.

BMI Series in Dialogic Organization Development

© 2020 Gervase Bushe

All rights reserved . No part of this publication may be reproduced, distributed, or transmitted in any form or by any means, including photocopying, recording, or other electronic or mechanical methods, without the prior written permission of the publisher, except in the case of brief quotations embodied in critical reviews and certain other non-commercial uses permitted by copyright law. For permission requests, write to the publisher addressed "Attention Permissions" at the address below

BMI Publishing
Bushe-Marshak Institute for Dialogic Organization Development
3898 Trenton Place
North Vancouver, BC
Canada V7R 3G5
www.b-m-institute.com

Library and Archives Canada Cataloguing in Publication
Title: The dynamics of generative change / Gervase R. Bushe, Ph.D. Names: Bushe, Gervase R., 1955 - author.
Description: Series statement: BMI series in dialogic organization development | Includes bibliographical references.
Identifiers: Canadiana 20190213132 | ISBN 9798689289847 (softcover)
Subjects: LCSH: Organizational change. | LCSH: Organizational learning.
Classification: LCC HD58.8 .B86 2020 | DDC 658.4/06—dc23

ISBN: 9798689289847
Imprint: BMI Publishing

Cover and interior design: Vancouver Desktop Publishing Center

Contents

Foreword By The Series Editors / 5

Introduction / 7

ONE
Identify the Adaptive Challenge / 16

TWO
Reframe into a Possibility Focused Purpose Statement / 33

THREE
Engage Stakeholders in Generative Conversations / 44

FOUR
Launch Self-Initiated Probes and Learn as You Go / 59

FIVE
Scale Up and Embed Successful Probes / 82

Conclusion / 92

APPENDIX
Robin's meeting notes from the First MT meeting / 97

References / 101

Foreword By The Series Editors

The term *Dialogic Organization Development* was first used in a 2009 article we published in *The Journal of Applied Behavioral Science*. In that article, we wanted to describe how we had seen organization development evolve and contrast it with the original form of OD, which we labeled Diagnostic OD. We were unhappy with how OD textbooks continued to treat the newer premises and practices as if they fit the earlier model. We wanted to create a space for people to think about, research, develop, and discuss these newer approaches to change. This book series is a continuation of that ambition and purpose.

Dialogic OD is a still developing mindset (rather than a set of specific methods). It is rooted in two key intellectual movements that are influencing all social science: how social reality is constructed, maintained, and changed by how we talk (post-modernism), and how social systems emerge and self-organize without leadership direction or a plan (complexity). We have written several articles and book chapters about this, and readers of this book (and all books in the series) are encouraged to access our website, www. B-M-Institute.com. Most of our writings and those of some others are available there for free. The articles and book chapters at the website provide a general overview of the theory of Dialogic OD, how it is the same and different from Diagnostic OD, and the basic ideas about leadership, consulting, change and creating great organizations embedded in Dialogic OD.

Since 2005 we have devoted much of our time and attention to conceptualizing and explaining Dialogic OD. Now we are turning our attention to encouraging presentations of specific dialogic practices applicable to all change methods and approaches. Each of the books in this series is a short, focused, and most important, practical exploration of one topic intended to continue expanding the theory and practice of Dialogic OD. We hope you enjoy the books. We welcome proposals for further volumes.

If you are relatively new to this set of ideas, you can download and read the free "Companion Booklet to the BMI series in Dialogic OD" by requesting it from the www.b-m-institute.com website.

Gervase R. Bushe
Robert J. Marshak
July 2019

Introduction

This book describes a process of change that has emerged over the past twenty years without being explicitly named or concretely described. It has shown up under a variety of labels, but often without all the necessary components identified or explained. Bob Marshak and I call it the Generative Change Model (Marshak & Bushe, 2018). I believe that it is the process of change that lies unseen or unspoken under a variety of Dialogic Organization Development and Large Group Intervention methods … when they are successful. I think once you see it, and understand it, it will be apparent how it resolves many of the problems inherent in traditional Planned Change Models. The Generative Change Model works with complexity, taps into the collective wisdom and motivation of those who will have to change to make a change, and produces transformational change results rapidly.

My purpose in writing this book is to:

- To help new organization development practitioners understand what needs to happen in a structured Dialogic OD process intended to produce transformational change.
- To help experienced organization development practitioners sharpen their planning and use of Dialogic OD.

In this introduction, I will briefly describe the dominant and widely used Planned Change Model and contrast it with the Generative Change Model (GCM). The rest of the book is organized around a case. While the names and some of the facts have been changed to disguise the organization and simplify the story, most of what is described in the case happened. Specifically, the adaptive challenge, the generative image, the design of the engagement events, the results that emerged, and the timeline in which they emerged, are an accurate description of a real generative change effort.

Each chapter follows the story of Consolidated Construction Material Supply and discusses, in order, the different phases in the GCM. Each chapter starts with the story and then pauses to discuss key issues in successfully applying the GCM. Each chapter concludes with a checklist of things to pay attention to when utilizing generative change.

The Dominant Planned Change Model

Some people reading this book will notice the title pays homage to the seminal "The Dynamics of Planned Change" (Lippitt, Watson and Westly, 1958). The processes described in that book are still what most managers and consultants inherently use to create change in organizations. Figure 1 is a common way of representing the planned change approach.

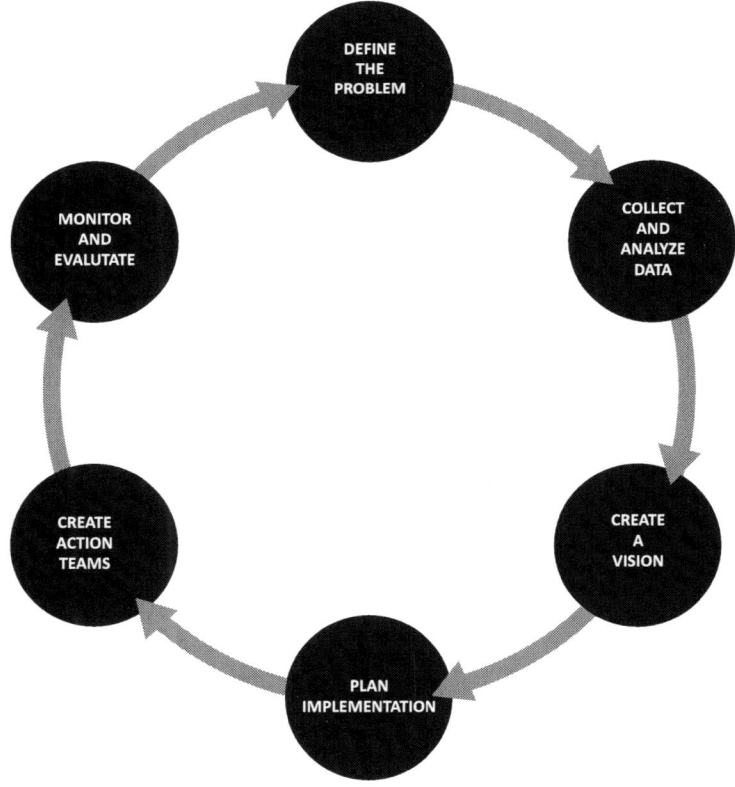

Figure 1: The Planned Change Model

In the planned change approach, you begin by defining the problem you want to solve. You involve experts, and sometimes employees, who collect and analyze data and understand the various facets of the problem. They may recommend solutions to the problem but, from the planned change perspective, success requires that leaders provide or sanction a clear <u>vision</u> of what the team, department or organization will look like when the change is implemented. In other words, we expect our leaders to say, "Here is the answer; follow me." An implementation plan follows, with more or less precisely defined targets. Implementation teams are formed to roll out the changes. In the better-managed changes, feedback processes are put in place to identify problems with the changes or implementation process, as they roll out, and propose solutions. Over the past 30 years, the discipline of change management has evolved and developed ever more complex processes for identifying, communicating and training employees on each facet of the change, taking into account all the interdependencies, accounting for cultural issues in the organization and cultural variations across the organization. The implicit theory is that if the solution to the problem (vision) is well thought through, and the changes required of each individual can be identified, and clearly communicated to those individuals, then implementation problems will only be a result of unmotivated employees or a lack of skill to do what's being asked of them.

The unpleasant truth, however, is that planned changes in organizations often fail, or at least fail to deliver what was intended. The handful of studies on success rates consistently find about 3 out of 4 fail (e.g., Eaton, 2010; Towers Watson, 2013). Why does the traditional approach to change so often fail?

Some of the widely discussed reasons include:

- Depending on one person, or a few people, to come up with the answer to complex, multi-faceted, and fluid problems.

- Experts who are not involved in day to day operations designing changes that don't work at the front lines, or create new problems.

- Hiring expensive consulting firms to propose an organizational redesign, but only being able to implement a portion of it, resulting in more problems than it solved.

- Hoping that using representatives of the various stakeholders to help design changes will reduce resistance to change, but it doesn't.
- By the time all the data is collected and analyzed, recommendations and decisions are made, the situation has changed.
- How everything, from how a problem is defined, to which recommendations are discussed, is as much a political process as a rational one.
- Getting front line people engaged and energized in proposing solutions only to create cynicism and demotivation from apparent lack of follow-through.
- The familiar experience that the only way to really transform an organization is to close it down and start over again, either through re-hiring selectively, or starting fresh someplace else.

In addition to all that, the most basic reason may be that most organizational problems are too complex for the planned change approach. One of the emerging themes in organization studies is a distinction between complicated and complex. Complicated problems can be figured out using rational, engineering-type processes, and you can come up with an answer that will likely solve the problem. Complex problems, however, have too many moving parts. There are so many interdependencies, and unknown contingencies, that it is not possible to reliably predict and engineer what the outcome of any set of decisions and actions will be.

For complicated, problems, the dominant "technical" managerial mindset has a good track record of success. This mindset looks at organizations in abstract terms as different processes and people that have to be engineered to fit together to produce products and services in a given environment. People are "human resources," or "talent," and organizations are made up of parts that can be re-organized, re-engineered, scaled up, downsized or outsourced. In this mindset, successful organizations require wise, heroic leaders with the right vision and a leadership team where rational decision-making leads individuals to take appropriate actions. In this view, organizational results come from applying generalizable tools and techniques (best practices) to the choices, intentions, and strategies of leaders and teams. While uncertainty and ambiguity are acknowledged, people then proceed to act, and encourage others to act, as if organizational outcomes are predictable.

This mindset does not appear very good at managing volatile, uncertain, complex, and ambiguous situations—which describes many organizational change scenarios. Ralph Stacey and his colleagues at the Hertfordshire Institute in the UK have persuasively argued, for many years, that this technical mindset does not capture the complexity of what happens when you have hundreds of different people engaged in a collective enterprise. Being able to adopt their "complex responsive processes of relating" view of organizations (Stacey, 2001; 2015) may be necessary to understand and work with generative change. From this point of view, organizations are understood as flows of conversations occurring at different times in different places by various actors and that what happens is mainly influenced by who talks with whom about what, when and how. Rather than being independent actors, everyone in an organization is highly interdependent regardless of how high up the pecking order and everyone is both constrained and enabled by others. Leaders can't control what anyone else thinks, feels, or wants, and leaders can often feel powerless to influence their organizations, regardless of their vision. Far from being purely rational, much of what takes place in organizations is propelled by emotion, particularly fear and anxiety, but also hope, inspiration, and pride. What's happening on the ground in any specific organization is so unique to it that generalizable tools and techniques usually have limited value. In the end, sometimes things we didn't expect happen, and sometimes things happen as expected, but mangers have very little control over what individuals think, feel, want, or do.

Table 1 lists some of the differences between the technical mindset and a complex responsive mindset. It is not a question of which one is "right." They are both right—they are different ways of seeing the same thing, and each leads to very different assumptions about leading, organizing, and organizational change. And they are probably both necessary to high performing organizations. The Generative Change Model is consistent with a complex responsive mindset.

Table 1: Technical versus Complex Responsive Mindsets

The Technical Mindset sees	but the Complex Responsive Mindset sees
organizations in the abstract, as systems, as 'things' and parts that can be moved around, subject to impersonal, environmental and technological forces,	organizations as conversations and that what happens is influenced by who talks with whom, about what, when, and how.
independent, autonomous, rational individuals making choices and taking action,	our interdependence and how we constrain and enable each other and can't get much done without the consent of others.
wise, heroic leaders whose vision and acumen steer their organizations to success,	how difficult it is to control what others choose and do, and how leaders often feel powerless to influence their organizations.
rational, analytical ways of making decisions, using big data and increasingly automated decision processes,	that far from being purely rational, people are emotional and often unconsciously driven by the anxieties aroused by organizational life.
generalizable tools and techniques of organizing and leadership in the belief that they will improve organizations,	situations so uncertain and the local contingencies so important that any generic tools have limited value.
results coming from the choices, intentions, and strategies made by leaders and teams,	results are emerging from the interplay of all the choices, intentions, and strategies of all the stakeholders in both intended and unintended ways.
uncertainty and ambiguity, but then proceeds to act, and encourages others to act, as if there was certainty and predictability, as if we could control large organizations.	that sometimes we are surprised, and sometimes we are not; we have very little control over people and we can never be certain about what anyone will do next.

Adapted from R. Stacey, 2015

The Generative Change Model

In the literature on how leaders can manage complexity, there are basically two solutions. One is to find ways to reduce the complexity to the level of complicated so that rational data-driven problem-solving models can be used. The other is to manage complexity by trying small experiments and seeing what works. The Generative Change Model is based on the second solution.

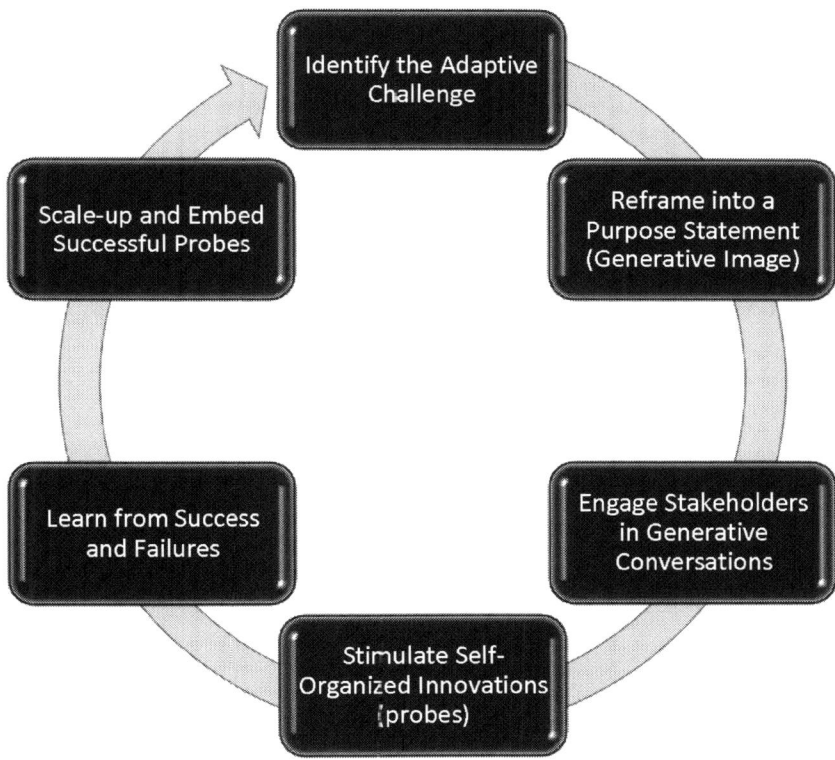

Figure 2: The Generative Change Model

The idea is that in complexity, it is not possible to understand what effects what except in retrospect. So to figure out what to do, try a little safe-fail experiment and see what happens. David Snowden calls these "probes" (Snowden & Boone, 2007), a term I will use in this book.

Collins and Hanson (2011) call this process "fire bullets, then cannonballs." Rather than assuming anyone is smart enough to anticipate all the possible permutations of all the factors influencing a situation ahead of time (the vision), assume you can't predict what will work. Instead, launch as many probes as possible and learn as you go. When something works, scale it up. There are many other names for probes, like experiments, pilot projects, prototypes, and so on. What you do, essentially, is to keep firing bullets until you hit something, then you bring in the cannon.

The Generative Change Model identifies the steps required to engage the people who will have to change (stakeholders), in conversations where they come up with new ideas (probes) they are willing to act on. They are encouraged to self-initiate action while leaders pay attention to what's working and what isn't. The good ideas and innovations are scaled up.

More importantly, the generative change process creates a more adaptive, agile organization, better able to tackle increasing complexity and produce far more change far more quickly than anyone familiar with planned change would consider reasonable. As shown in Figure 2, Generative Change begins by identifying the "adaptive challenge" that leaders are willing to put time, effort and resources into managing. I say managing because adaptive challenges are never "solved"—which is a major reason why spending a lot of time and resources identifying "the vision" is generally not useful. Chapter 1 describes this in more detail.

In chapter 2, we'll look at how that adaptive challenge needs to be reframed into a future-focused purpose statement that will speak to the variety of stakeholders who will have to change to manage the adaptive challenge. In that chapter, we will look at the difference between purpose and vision, and describe the most powerful kind of purpose statement, what I call a "generative image." Some advice on how to create generative images is provided.

With a powerful purpose statement in hand, leaders then invite the stakeholders (literally, everyone who has a stake in the issue) into "generative conversations"—these are conversations that will produce new ideas that people who produced them will want to act on. In chapter 3, I describe some of the things you need to consider in the design of "engagement events" that will power a generative change process. One is that they lead people to self-organize into small teams that leave an engagement event ready to launch a probe.

In chapter 4, we'll look at the process of launching probes and what is required to ensure learning occurs from successful and failed experiments while creating an adaptive, agile organizational culture. In chapter 5, we'll look at how much change is possible from amplifying probes in a way that leads to a truly transformed organization. The Conclusion briefly discusses some of the issues that can come up in a generative change process that did not appear in this case.

ONE

Identify the Adaptive Challenge

The first job when you enter as a Dialogic OD consultant is to listen deeply (Marshak, 2020) to understand the flow of conversations that are taking place among the key players. Try to understand how they make sense of their dilemmas, what their hopes and fears are, and get a sense of the challenge(s) that have them stuck. This is often different from the original "presenting problem".

We begin the case of the Material Supply group at Consolidated Construction from the first phone call from Charlie, the Director of Material Supply, to Robin, the OD consultant.

Consolidated Construction Material Supply (CCMS)

> "Three years ago, I joined the company as manager of Regional Warehousing. Three months ago, I was promoted to Director of Material Supply. We have a lot of problems that are causing significant daily turmoil, and I don't think we can solve our problems until we increase the amount of cooperation between the different units in the organization. I was at a talk you gave a few years ago on collaboration in organizations and what you said made sense to me. I thought maybe you could help us out."

That was part of the initial phone call from Charlie Boyd, Director of Material Supply for Consolidated Construction, a large, residential and commercial builder in the Pacific Northwest that had been operating for over 50 years. He had contacted Robin Bhodi, a local OD consultant, seeking help with some changes to the Material Supply organization. Later that week they met at Charlie's office near the Central Warehouse, and he described an organization with so many issues that part of the problem was figuring out where to start. About three years earlier Consolidated had hired one of the large, global consulting firms to develop a strategy and organizational structure for its entire supply chain, of which Material Supply was a part. Charlie's perception was that the consulting firm had copied the strategy and design of one of the better run, large construction firms and presented that as a blueprint for Consolidated without really tailoring it to the unique characteristics of the company. In the past three years only about 40% of the recommendations had been implemented, and the consequence was that there were a lot of internal processes that didn't work together well, an antiquated IT system, areas of supply where it wasn't clear who was in charge, issues with how construction crews ordered and received materials and general low morale throughout.

Charlie described the structure of Material Supply (CCMS), with nearly 200 employees, as three functional units that were interdependent but tended to operate in isolation from each other (See Figure 3). He attributed that to the previous Director's more hierarchal leadership style that did not create an environment of integration and teamwork

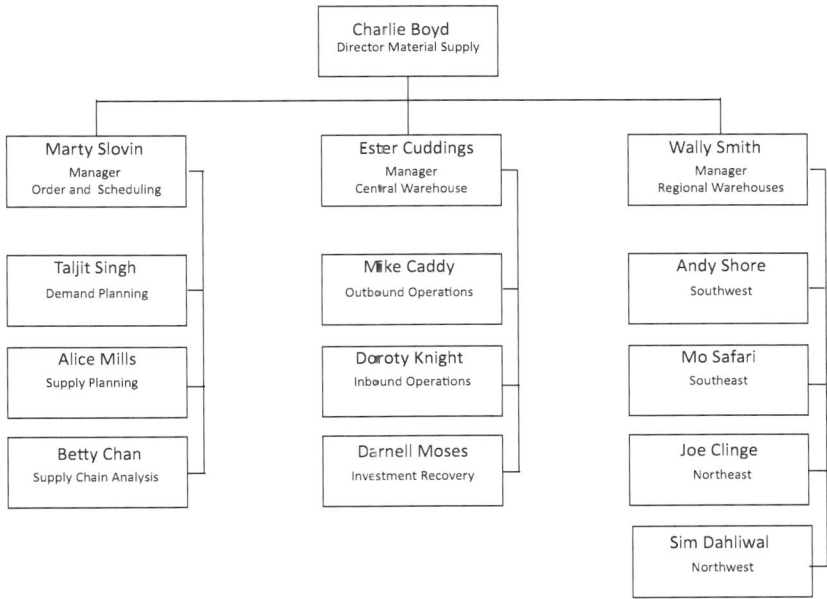

Figure 3: Managerial Structure of CCMS

across the managers of the various operations. The three units included Order and Scheduling (O&S) which was responsible for estimating what materials Consolidated would need in the next 6-12 months and making sure they didn't run out while keeping costs of goods on hand as low as possible. The Central Warehouse (CW) was where most of the materials Consolidated bought, from nails to lumber, to furnaces, tools and electrical, were initially shipped to, inspected, stored, and from where the Regional Warehouses made weekly orders that CW had to pack and ship as accurately and economically as possible. Regional Warehousing (RW), was a group of smaller materials distribution points scattered throughout the many small communities in the four states Consolidated operated in, and from which the construction crews got most of their materials.

Charlie: We are a pretty hierarchical company, and people are used to a top-down management style. Most of our senior managers are engineers, and the company's approach to change is to have experts design the change and then tell managers to implement it. But our workforce is unionized, long-time employees, so it's difficult to mandate changes if they don't like them. The experience with the reorganization of the supply chain was pretty typical. We've been through different change management programs, and the perception at the front lines is that if you duck your head they go away. There's a certain amount of cynicism throughout the organization.

Robin: What are you hoping we can accomplish?

Charlie: I don't think anything will get better without more collaboration between the three units. I've been holding monthly meetings with my management team, and I think my managers are starting to open up and trust each other. The previous manager never held team meetings, but now people are starting to communicate freely and I think they are interested in trying to make things better.

Robin: What about further down the organization?

Charlie: Supervisors and employees below them, and people in the rest of the organization? Well, they are still pretty guarded

Robin: and cautious. What do you think we have to do to increase collaboration and engagement?

Robin: My philosophy is based on something called Dialogic OD, which is a more bottom-up approach to change. I don't think you increase collaboration by talking about it—instead, we have to find real opportunities for motivated people to collaborate. To do that, your team needs to identify one or more issues that people really care about and bring them into well-designed conversations with each other. The fundamental principle is that the people who have to make any change work have to be invited to the conversation. Those conversations need to be organized to encourage people to propose changes that they want to act on. Some probably won't work out and that's OK. The important thing is to encourage bottom-up action and learn as you go.

Charlie (with a twinkle in his eye) THAT would be very counter-cultural in Consolidated, but it fits with the way I want to do things and with some of the stuff I've been learning in the MBA program I'm close to finishing. I think we should begin by having you come to our next management team meeting

The First MT meeting

After Charlie introduced Robin to the group, Robin asked, "why are we here?" and then sat back and listened for the better part of an hour as the group discussed its issues. Marty started by describing their inability to get the construction crews to follow the rules for ordering materials and how that caused headaches for different people in different ways.

Marty: A crew will come to a regional warehouse and ask for some material they see right in front of them. But they didn't order it like they should have so if the keeper (a unionized employee who works at a regional warehouse) gives it to them someone else who did order it is going to be out of luck. In some cases, the keeper will say no, so the crew lead will call their boss who will call someone else and the next thing you know the keeper is being yelled at by someone way

	up the food chain, so he ends up giving the crew what they wanted. So, a lot of our keepers give them what they want and then have to scramble to cover it.
Ester:	Yeah, or a keeper will call Central Warehouse needing a rush shipment of something, and the person they get on the phone will tell them they have to follow the procedures, so the keeper will call someone else, and keep calling around until they find someone who will rush them the material.
Marty:	We have rules and processes for how things should be ordered and shipped, but people break the rules all the time. If we could just get people to follow the procedures, 90% of our problems would go away.
Wally:	Well, one of the problems is that the rules keep changing, and no one is really clear on who is supposed to be setting the rules. Is Material Supply responsible for planning and managing materials flow, or are we just supposed to do what construction tells us? Whenever we've pushed back, the organization tells us we are responsible and we should manage it, but then something comes up, and some Vice-President is yelling at some poor schmuck in a warehouse to release material.

After listening to the complaints for a while, Robin spoke up.

Robin:	I get the impression you would like to manage the operation like a well-oiled machine, but the complexity and variability of the demands made on you make that difficult. Maybe it's the nature of the situation and is too complex and variable to use standardization as the solution.
Ester:	Like maybe we should become more nimble and customer-focused?

The group became quiet for a few moments and then Marty spoke up.

Marty:	Nah, there are lots of ways we can increase standardization and make life saner.
Charlie:	I would even say that the lack of simple standard ways of doing things is a key source of pain for our employees. It's gotten to the point that success equals did I avoid getting yelled at today. That's what's causing morale to sink and people to stop caring.

Robin: OK then, a basic principle of organizing is that if you want to use standardization to manage things, you have to buffer your operating core from uncertainty[1]. So in addition to users who show up asking for things you aren't expecting, and not following procedures, what else causes unpredictable variability for you?"

As they discussed the question, Robin privately noted the following things:

External Factors

- The partial implementation of the supply chain reorganization has created areas of uncertainty about who is responsible for what.
- Items arrive for warehousing in different sizes and at unpredictable times.
- Lack of clarity of the role of CCMS in managing some vendor contracts.
- Other units in Consolidated make purchasing decisions and sign up vendors on some materials so they have little control over how those vendors act.
- How crews/contractors order things vary.
- Architects who don't understand Consolidated's materials policies using the wrong materials or creating plans that have the wrong materials showing up at the wrong place at the wrong time.
- Crews/contractors saying they want something by some date, but then needing it at a different date.
- Crews/contractors use multiple points of contact within CCMS to make demands and get service, which creates more confusion about who is responsible for what internally.

Internal Factors

- Not buying in time to meet a purchase order.
- Materials stocked incorrectly or mislabeled.

---

1 Thompson, J. (1967) *Organizations in Action.* NY: McGraw-Hill.

- Inaccurate waybills.
- Different employees reacting to different user demands differently.
- Some lack of clarity about which units have authority/responsibility for certain decisions.
- The number of acting supervisors currently in the regional warehouses.
- The IT system deals with partial orders, stockouts, and backorders differently, causing lots of confusion for keepers.
- Different keepers have different procurement strategies and "game the system".

After this hour-long discussion, Marty was visibly agitated . . .

Marty: Look, some of the time stuff happens the way it's supposed to happen, we just don't know how often, but I'd guess its 40-60% of the time. Sure, there is a certain percentage of requests we are going to get that we can't predict, that will always be there, but I'm certain it's not that much. I'm certain we can get to the point where 90% of our work happens the way it is supposed to happen if we can just define the right processes and make people use them.

Robin: How has that worked for you in the past?

Everyone in the group snorted and shook their heads, indicating that it hadn't worked very well.

Robin: Did you include the people who would have to live by the rules, like the construction crews, in those conversations?"

Ester: We even had the Vice-President of Construction involved in developing and signing off on the procedures and then the very next week he was yelling at some guy in the warehouse to screw the process and ship something.

Robin: I can understand why a construction manager doesn't want his crew standing around because they've run out of material. My hunch is that most people in CCMS would rather be able to say yes to your users than enforce rules.

Ester: That's true, but right now so much is out of control and we understand so little about it. For example, before the meeting Mike told me we couldn't complete an order to Bellingham because there aren't any slag bolts on the shelves, but our inventory system is telling us we have four months' supply.

Marty: Yeah, that's because some keepers are hoarding it.

Charlie: Maybe, but there's a reason keepers hoard materials, wouldn't you say Wally?

The group continued for the next fifteen minutes or so to discuss current examples of ways in which people from the three units did things "outside the rules" a) to get their job done and b) because they didn't fully trust the other units.

They then turned to a discussion about what to focus their efforts on. Robin said they needed to have a central question they were trying to answer, which they could then come at in different ways. The group discussed this for a while and with Marty's urging they created this question: **How do we create less volatility and greater clarity/agreement so we can achieve 90% of our work within planned/agreed to guidelines?**

Robin was curious how much latitude they had to experiment and try different things. What kinds of expectations did Charlie face from his bosses? It turned out that Charlie's boss was a very hands-off kind of guy, and the only expectations they thought they faced were to stay within headcount and keep the construction crews satisfied.

As the meeting came to the end of its allotted time, Robin described how Dialogic OD works by engaging everyone who will be affected by a change (stakeholders) in new conversations to generate ideas people will act on. To do that requires leaders to guide the process of change but engage those stakeholders who have to make the change in proposing and trying out solutions, and then see what works. There seemed to be some buy-in to that, but Robin also sensed some hesitation and acknowledgment that it would not be common practice at Consolidated Construction.

With Robin's guidance, they decided that at the next meeting they would identify

1. Who, exactly, would need to change to make any such changes work?

In other words, which employees, and possibly people outside CCMS and Consolidated, need to be involved in proposing solutions?

2. What kinds of change processes would be most likely to succeed given the issues, culture, players and situational opportunities and constraints CCMS faces?

The other thing Robin left them with was a request that they think about how their core question could be rephrased in a way that would make it a compelling question to employees, the kind of question that "people would be willing to crawl over glass to be in conversation about."

They agreed to meet again for a half-day in the next two weeks. Robin went back to his office, typed up his notes on what he had heard during the meeting and sent them to Charlie, asking him if he had missed anything. Charlie distributed them to the rest of the team with the same question. No one had any revisions, and a couple of the managers remarked to Charlie that Robin seemed to "get it". This became a pattern for all subsequent meetings.

—Pause in the story—

Entry for Dialogic OD[2]

As a Dialogic OD consultant, you are entering into a stream of conversations that have been going on for a long time. Your first job (besides developing a trusting relationship) is to get a sense of what those conversations are, how people are making sense of the situation, how they frame their problems and opportunities[3], and, most importantly, what they care about. To do that you need to ask some questions that stimulate the client to be in conversation with each other, not with you. In conventional consulting, most people are trained to lead a meeting where you facilitate the group to define the problem. However, when the conversation is focused on the consultant the discussion tends to become more abstract and people mouth formulaic responses. If you take on a kind of project manager role, the tendency is to quickly construct a

---

2 If you are not familiar with the theory of Dialogic OD, you might want to first read the free pamphlet available from B-M-Institute.com
3 See Marshak's book on Dialogic Process Consulting, in this series, for more about this kind of "deep listening".

narrative about what is going on, and what the work with the client will be, without much thought about how the group is constructing their social reality.

During the meeting described here, people seldom talked to Robin; they were talking to each other. Robin asked the occasional question and made the occasional observation but mostly he was listening closely. This is a profound form of inquiry, even though it isn't "diagnosis". Besides an opening (in this case, "why are we here?") a Dialogic OD consultant won't have a pre-set list of questions to ask. They won't have any particular model they are assessing the client against, even though they should have a wealth of theoretical knowledge about organizations, organizing, and change that informs what they are hearing. In one sense this is an entry and scouting process. The consultant is entering into the system to get a sense of what is going on and paying attention to how issues are framed and discussed that may be causing them to be stuck. She or he is paying attention to the energy in the room, and what affects it. However, the consultant is not at any point going to tell them what s/he thinks the problem is. Instead, the consultant wants to help them engage with each other to discuss the multiple sets of issues and challenges without making any one focal.

Since the consultant will be doing less talking and facilitating than usual, people will naturally be wondering what is going on in the consultant's mind. It's not unusual for clients to project their sense of inadequacy onto the consultant and imagine that he or she is judging them. Robin's solution to this was to write the meeting minutes where he described his thoughts about the meeting. You can see a copy of the notes Robin sent from this meeting in the Appendix.

What Does the Sponsor Care About?

It's not unusual to be called in to help with a change project by someone who doesn't have enough power and authority to sponsor that change project. Sometimes these are change agents—people who are championing a change but don't have authority over the people they are trying to change. In that case, the first thing you have to do is to work with the change agent to meet with and engage the necessary sponsor(s) (More on sponsors in Chapter 5). Working on any significant change effort requires the support of the people who have the authority and/

or control the resources that will be necessary to succeed in the change. In this case, Robin questioned the group to see if Charlie's boss needed to be involved, or whether other parts of the organization could stand in the way of any changes they'd want to make to their processes and procedures and was satisfied that Charlie had the authority to sponsor this change.

To identify the adaptive challenge that the sponsor will be willing to put the necessary effort and energy into, you have to get a sense of what they want more of, what a desirable future would look like for them and the people they lead. I also believe that for sustainable change you need to tie this to important organizational outcomes. In this case, Charlie's "presenting problem" was that he wanted more collaboration between the three units. I don't think talking about issues of organizing, (e.g., talking about more collaboration, better communications, better decision-making, increased inclusion and diversity), rather than a focus on the group's purpose, are good candidates for generative change projects. For one, I don't think you get more collaboration by talking about collaboration. There will probably be lots of well-intentioned talk but not much change in behavior back on the job. For change to stick, people have to experience improvement at work. Holding generative conversations and launching probes that only have the intent to improve collaboration will soon surface the question, "collaboration for what?". Instead, you create collaboration by focusing people on a common purpose (discussed more in the next chapter) and creating opportunities for them to work collaboratively. The Dialogic OD practitioner has to help the leadership team get underneath the surface concerns (like more collaboration) to find out "collaboration for what?". What deeply concerns this leader or leadership team? And why are they stuck? So, at the same time that you are doing scouting and entry, you are hosting a process of self-study on their part, asking questions that stimulate their conversation so that they are having a different conversation than what they are used to. If they are not a) having a different conversation that b) they find useful, then you are not doing your job.

This is similar to Diagnostic OD in that the intent is to increase their awareness and their choicefulness, and produce the core outcomes of OD enunciated 50 years ago by Chris Argyris (1970): a) help people get valid and useful information on which b) they can base free and informed choices that c) they are personally committed to. We are not there in a doctor-patient relationship, nor as a content expert, but as a process expert who knows something about organizational change and can guide others in making free and informed choices about how to change their organization.

What's different is that:

1. The Dialogic OD practitioner sees inquiry and change occurring simultaneously. In diagnostic OD first we do an inquiry, then we decide what to change. In Dialogic OD, they occur at the same time. In this case we see how, in the process of having these conversations, the mental maps and the culture of the team are starting to change. They are questioning their standard operating procedures and opening up to doing things differently.

2. We are not interested in arriving at a problem statement, a definition of the situation or a diagnosis to move forward. I think all that does is privilege one way of looking at things over other, just as valid, ways of looking at things. If anything, we want to encourage the variety and complexity of the situation to be surfaced, both as a disruptive force (you can't create developmental change (Bushe & Ngaishi, 2018) without disruption) and to ensure that we don't create overly simplistic solutions. What we are interested in, however, is finding an image of a desirable future that encompasses the complexity and will capture what is most important to the people who will ultimately have to make the change happen.

The Nature of Adaptive Challenges

Ron Heifetz (1994) coined the term adaptive challenge to distinguish this kind of issue from "technical problems". It is similar to what others have called "wicked problems" (Churchman, 1967) and "complex decision situations" {Snowden and Boone, 2007). Table 2 describes some of the important differences between adaptive challenges and technical problems

Table 2: Technical Problems and Adaptive Challenges

TECHNICAL PROBLEMS	ADAPTIVE CHALLENGES
Easy to operationally define.	Difficult to agree on what the "problem" is.
Lend themselves to operational (process and procedures) solutions.	Require changes in values, beliefs, relationships, and mindsets.
People are generally receptive to technical solutions they understand.	People generally resist adopting other-defined values and beliefs.
Often can be solved by authorities or experts.	The stakeholders have to be involved in solving it.
Requires change in just one or a few places; often contained within organizational boundaries.	Requires change in numerous places; usually across organizational boundaries.
Solutions can often be implemented relatively quickly by changing rules or work processes.	Adaptation requires experiments and discoveries as well as wrong turns and dead ends.
Technical problems stay solved until something else changes.	Adaptation creates new problems that will have to be adapted to.

Source: Bushe & Nagaishii, 2018

Adaptive problems are complex decision situations where, by definition, there are too many sources of uncertainty and variability to be able to predict what will cause what. Some people argue that as soon as humans are involved you have a complex problem, because it's difficult to predict how people will make sense of things, and what the result of any meeting or communication will be (Shaw, 2002; Stacy, 2015). There are lots of instances where using a problem-solving approach and applying technical expertise is useful and appropriate. Most of us wouldn't want people to design airplanes by trying stuff out and seeing what happens. Table 3 provides some examples of technical problems and related adaptive challenges.

Table 3 Examples of Technical Problems and Adaptive Challenges

Complicated, Technical Problem	Complex, Adaptive Challenge
How do we identify potential safety issues and implement safe operating procedures?	How do we develop a safety culture from top to bottom and across all operations?
How do we maximize the utilization of mobile equipment?	How do we introduce new digital technology that will minimize the need for staff?
How do we ensure nurses know the safest methods for lifting patients?	How do we improve the health and wellness of nurses?
How do we ensure accurate information is provided during handoffs from sales to installation?	How do we increase collaboration between sales and operations?
How do we reduce errors in medications delivered to patients?	How do we get patients to take more responsibility for taking their meds?

Most managers have been trained to approach all change issues like technical problems, using a planned change approach, and this causes many of the failed organizational change efforts. You can see that at play in the case. By the end of the first meeting, Marty has influenced the group to define the issue to work on as a technical problem: "How do we create less volatility and greater clarity/agreement so we can achieve 90% of our work within planned/agreed to guidelines?" This is pretty normal, but notice they also agree that trying to manage their problems with getting the right materials to the right place at the right time through expertise and problem-solving has not worked in the past. There are many sources of uncertainty that are out of their control. Part of them knows this won't work, but in the early stages of a Dialogic OD project they don't know how else to think about it.

Normally, adaptive challenges involve one or more of the following three dilemmas:

They require managing paradoxes—that is to successfully manage the adaptive challenge requires doing things that seem to be contradictory.

Human beings will never develop a definitive solution to how to divide up work and then coordinate that work, conclusively, since effective collective action rests on a set of tensions. Paradoxes (Smith and Berg, 1987), polarities (Johnson, 1992) and competing values (Quinn, 1988) are different ways of describing these tensions. Quinn (1988)'s competing values model, for instance, tells us that organizational effectiveness depends on both managing outside and managing inside, of having enough stability and having enough flexibility. It necessitates adapting to external demands while at the same time, standardizing internal operations. Working through people and relationships and working through impersonal processes and routines are both necessary.

To properly identify the adaptive challenge, you have to understand the dilemmas the organization is facing. In this case, we can see some common dilemmas and a couple of unique ones (some of these will become more obvious in the next chapter):

- Holding down costs AND giving customers what they want
- Meeting customer needs AND prescribing customer behavior
- Managing people through tasks AND managing tasks through people
- Managing workflow through rules AND managing workflow through relationships
- Stability and control AND adaptability and resilience

And two somewhat unique to CCMS:

- If you follow the rules you get beat up AND if you don't follow the rules you get beat up.
- Servicing crews as the source of all problems and stress AND servicing crews as the source of all motivation and pride

They require changing the leaders' mindsets—that is, to successfully manage the adaptive challenge requires thinking differently than the leaders currently think

A key dilemma for this group of leaders, and this is often the reason a consultant is brought in, is that they don't know how to address the problems they are confronting. They normally bring an engineering approach to problems of organizing, and it's expected in their organization. They are used to experts designing solutions to problems and leaders telling employees what to do. Part of this change process will be a learning journey for them.

Over the whole of this case, the most difficult habit to break was to spend time in management meetings discussing solutions to problems, instead of how they would engage the people with the problems in solving them. By the time Robin exited they had learned to see their job was problem-setting, not solving, and got better at catching themselves and stopping their impulse to "fix it", but that impulse is strong. And why not? People mainly get promoted because they are good at problem-solving and like to do it. Other people expect this of them—"Hey boss, what should I do?". If the boss can't tell you, why is she the boss? All leaders have to do some problem solving, but adaptive challenges are not solved by a group of managers, or experts, sitting around a table. What is needed, and we go into this in-depth in the next chapter, are leaders who say, "I don't know what the answer is, but I know what our purpose needs to be and I invite you to bring your best game to pursuing that purpose."

They require embracing the idea that there are no timeless solutions to problems of organizing because any solution will inevitably create a new problem

As I stated above, organizing includes numerous polarities, contradictions, and paradoxes. Things that appear to be opposites are both necessary for organizational effectiveness. Organizational effectiveness is bi-polar, and today's solution will be an unavoidable cause of new problems to be solved tomorrow. We try decentralization after too much centralization, which will then create a need for more centralization. We hold on to routines until they become stifling and then depend on relationships until they become too inefficient, in a never-ending journey for how to best adapt to the various challenges the world keeps throwing at us.

A very important implication of this is that there is little value in spending a lot of time trying to figure out what the right answer is, and then try to get others to "buy-in". The generative change model suggests instead, surface and run with any answer that the people who will have to change are willing to implement. Generative change is a series of small wins, learning as you go, building on successes and learning from failures. As you go, conditions will change: the environment will change, the people involved will change, the very things you do will cause the conditions to change so that solutions that would not have worked last year may work now (and vice versa).

Another very important implication of this is that creating an adaptive, agile, learning organization is probably the most important objective of Dialogic Organization Development. We do this by working on specific problems in an agile, adaptive way. An important spin-off benefit is that by engaging stakeholders in the generative change process, we are developing the organization's capacity to more quickly and successfully take on the next adaptive challenge, as we shall see happened at CCMS.

Checklist for Starting a Generative Change Project

- ✓ Have you got the sponsorship you will need to work on that adaptive challenge? If not, how will you work up and out to get it?
- ✓ If the leader or group is not familiar with generative change, are they ready to let go of their usual ways of doing things?
- ✓ Are they prepared to let go of control and work with a more emergent form of change?
- ✓ Is it clear enough what adaptive challenge leaders are ready to put time and effort into?

TWO

Reframe into a Possibility Focused Purpose Statement

It isn't always necessary to develop a clear definition of the adaptive challenge as there can be many different ways of naming it. It also isn't always necessary for the sponsor or sponsoring group to be aware of all the dilemmas they are enmeshed with. How much that needs to be articulated and discussed will depend on the kind of people you are dealing with (some will want to think deeply about these issues, and others will want to "get on with it"). But the OD practitioner needs to have a pretty good idea of what it is so she or he can guide the next, critically important step in the generative change model—articulating the purpose that will guide the change effort. For this, the sponsor does need to agree on the exact wording of the purpose. The most effective is something called a "generative image".

The Second MT meeting

Robin came into the second meeting convinced that they needed to revise their key question into something people would care about, and hopefully, create a generative image. He started by asking them how they could revise the objective of "reducing volatility so more work could be executed according to plan" into something people in the organization cared about and would want to participate in changing. Intriguingly, however, they ignored his question and instead had a long discussion, amongst themselves, where Robin mainly listened. As Robin listened, he became aware that they were mainly talking about how to change the expectations and behaviors of construction crews and contractors. As the conversation unfolded, he realized they were talking themselves out of their usual way of doing things.

During this conversation, Robin privately noted several key beliefs that surfaced:

- Attempts in the past to manage user expectations through developing rules/service agreements had not worked.
- Rules had been created that didn't meet the crews' requirements.
- The largest percentage of demand was known and could be planned for, but a percentage of demand was unpredictable and was the source of problems. How much of each percentage was unclear.
- More of the unpredictable demand came from contractors; demand from Consolidated crews was much more predictable. Unpredictable demand from Consolidated crews was mainly a result of their customers making unpredictable changes, and the weather.
- Consolidated's new CEO wanted to improve the customer focus of the entire organization and increase employee engagement throughout the organization.
- Regional warehouses break the rules to more effectively service crews and hide how they do that from the central office.
- There is a tension in the organization between servicing crews and controlling costs, which plays out functionally with Regional Warehouses most oriented to servicing crews, O&S most oriented to managing costs, and CW in-between.
- There is a belief that increasing the amount of material stocked won't solve the problems created by unpredictable demand.

Wally: You guys know about Bob Tuttle?

Neither Ester nor Marty had ever heard of this particular keeper, though Charlie, having been the RW manager previously, knew him.

Wally: Bob never has a problem servicing his crews. He has an extremely well-organized inventory process, creates no problems for CW, and provides exemplary service to his

	crews and contractors in one of our most complex service areas.
Marty:	Well, I guess that's why I never heard of him.
Ester:	That sort of says a boatload about us, doesn't it?
Charlie:	How does he do it?"
Wally:	I don't know.
Robin:	One option we have is to engage the organization in studying how people in CCMS like Bob are effective.

This led to a conversation about how little knowledge sharing took place within CCMS. This, in turn, led to a discussion of the onboarding process at CCMS and how little it ensured people in one area understood the work of other areas. It surfaced that the nature and extent of onboarding differed across the different units of CCMS and that it mainly focused on ensuring people knew their jobs, but probably didn't provide much of an overview to CCMS as a whole.

Robin:	Do people from different parts of CCMS ever get together and is that useful?
Charlie:	We get a lot of the organization together for our annual safety meeting, and I think it's very useful for more than just safety.
Ester:	Oh, for sure, any meetings where people from different regions and units get together have spin-off benefits.
Wally:	Yeah, we should maybe do more of that.
Robin:	If you are going to use a generative change strategy, you will have to bring people from different units and regions together. It might be necessary to also bring in people from other units outside CCMS, and maybe even suppliers. But before we design those meetings, we need to reframe your issue into something that people who will have to change care about. So, I'm going to use this flipchart and I need you to help me identify what do your employees care about?

Robin stood at a flip chart that was in the meeting room and facilitated as they came up with the following five (in bold below):

1. **People in CCMS are motivated to ensure the crews have the materials they need.** Managers thought that the closer CCMS employees are to interacting with crews, the stronger this motivation.

2. **People care about being part of the CC team.** Managers believed there was a real interest in having good quality relationships with their colleagues scattered around the Pacific Northwest. In many of the small communities, there is palpable pride in being a Consolidated Construction employee and a feeling of being "part of the team" with the construction crews in their region.

3. **People care about doing things right.** The managers thought that not only do they want to supply crews, but they want to provide the right material at the right time to the right people. They want to feel pride in their work, not the source of others' frustration. Those who provide materials are motivated to give people what they ask for and ignore the rules. Those who try to stick to the rules find themselves over-turned by others inside or outside CCMS.

4. **People don't want to be yelled at all the time.** Managers thought there was too much panic mode, and this was a major impediment to employee morale. Mostly, people just wanted a stress free workday.

5. **People care about being heard.**

Robin: We need to identify the purpose that is going to guide our change process. Let me explain what I mean. A vision is like a goal or a target—something we are stretching toward. But a purpose is something we are trying to do every day. Usually, there is a plan for how to achieve a goal, but there can be lots of different ways to accomplish a purpose. As I've listened to you, it seems to me like your purpose is to get the right materials to the right people at the right time—would you agree?

Charlie: Yeah, I would say that is exactly it.

Robin: The problem with that purpose statement is that it doesn't open up many new avenues for thinking or talking—it's what people here have been thinking and talking about forever. To energize a change process, we need to frame a purpose that captures what people care about, and what you want more of, but does it in a way that's new and compelling. I call it short and sweet—short enough I will immediately get it, and sweet enough that people are compelled to get engaged.

After some discussion and a few ideas that didn't catch on, Ester spoke up.

Ester: How about our purpose is "stress-free work"?

Robin: That's better, but the problem with that is it doesn't focus the conversation enough on all the variables you want people to consider. I mean, they could decide the way to avoid being stressed is to ignore customer needs—you wouldn't want that would you?

Ester: No, of course not

Marty: How about "creating processes that work 90% of the time"?

Robin: Do you think that people will find that an exciting topic to engage in?

The group quickly agreed that would not do it. The discussion wove back and forth between identifying what they wanted more of, and what they were trying to do every day that people cared about, and finding a way to name it that would be exciting to employees.

Charlie: How about "stress-free customer service"?

As soon as Charlie said that people either pushed back in their chairs or leaned forward.

Wally: That's exactly what we want more of!

—Pause in the story—

From Adaptive Challenge to Purpose

A purpose is different from a vision or goal, and it is essential to successful generative change. By vision, I mean a clear idea of the future state you want to achieve. Leaders who can provide a convincing vision of a desirable future, and the path to get there, will attract followership. Vision is necessary for top-down, planned change processes to have any chance of success. But they are too much of a straight-jacket for the emergent, generative approach to change. A purpose, on the other hand, is a statement of what the group or organization is trying to do every day. It can often describe a state you may never attain, like eradicating poverty or or zero defects.

. Table 4 provides some examples of the difference between goals/visions and purposes.

Table 4. The Difference Between Vision and Purpose

A vision describes what you will be doing sometime in the future	A purpose describes what you are trying to do every day
We will operate in all 50 states by 2025	Grow the business
We will provide 100% on-time delivery in the next two years	Delight our customers
We will eliminate all scratches on door panels in the next two weeks	Reduce defects

There are at least two reasons for why a purpose, rather than a vision, is needed for generative change

Purpose provides more room for experiments and self-initiated action

A vision is a specific way to attain a purpose. A leader or leadership group has decided that this is the best way to attain that purpose, and now others have to line up behind that vision (buy the vision, get on the bus, etc.). There is much less room for experimentation, and for tapping into the creativity and intrinsic motivations in the people who will have to change. One hundred percent on-time delivery is only one way to delight customers, and may not be the most important thing to some customers. What happens to all the ideas that front line employees, who deal with customers every day have for how to delight customers? How much less committed to delighting customers will they feel if they are being stressed by a 100% on-time delivery promise, especially if it's for customers who have other priorities that can't be satisfied because of constraints from on-time delivery? Top-down mandated visions imply an implicit or explicit belief that employees are not committed to the purpose and if left to themselves, won't act in ways that further the purpose; or that they don't know how to accomplish the purpose and so must be directed. If either or both are true, a generative change process will not work. But when people are committed to a purpose, they will find ways to accomplish it—often different from what others might do—and that is the engine of innovation and learning.

Purpose makes successful use of emergence possible

When people have a common purpose, they are far more likely to self-organize in a way that supports the collective good. When they don't have a common purpose, they are more likely to self-organize in a way that supports their individual needs, wants, and agendas. Inherent in leaders' hesitation to use loosely guided, emergent change processes, is a belief that people mainly look after themselves and not the organization's needs. But when people care about accomplishing the same thing, left to themselves, they will self-organize in the best way they know how to succeed. In this case, you don't have a motivation problem, but you may need to upgrade people's knowledge or skills, and you often have to remove barriers that are getting in their way of doing what they know needs doing.

Generative Images

A generative image (Bushe, 1998, 2013; Bushe & Storch, 2015) is a combination of words that are new or unusual in the group in which they are used. To be generative, an image needs three qualities. One, it allows people to see a situation in a new way, allows for new conversations to take place that hadn't taken place before. It opens up people to think about options that hadn't occurred to them in the past and by doing so, creates pathways for new decisions and new behaviors. A very generative image has a second attribute. It is compelling; people want to act in the new way the image points toward. There needs to be something about the words that is attractive to people, even if they aren't sure what it means. It motivates new conversations and new actions. Third, generative images are ambiguous and hard to define even as they are attractive—this allows them to be a continuous source of new ideas. Generative image is one of the three core change processes in Bushe & Marshak's (2014) theory of Dialogic OD.

The generative image they landed on, in this case, was *stress-free customer service*. The "stress-free" part played to the desire for increased standardization, predictability, and control, (and not getting yelled at) while the customer service part played to the desire to be able to say "yes" to any request. It worked internally, as RW was the customer of

CW and both were the customer of O&S, as well as working externally in the sense that construction crews and contractors were customers of CCMS. To work, it was important that any change they made to reduce one group's stress could not be at the expense of increasing some other group's stress. It identified a purpose that was desirable to everyone in CCMS while encompassing the complexity of issues they needed to manage. At the same time, it was not obvious what stress-free customer service entailed—it had the necessary ambiguity to be able to spin off innovations for a long time to come.

Calling meetings to discuss how to increase stress-free customer service made it easy to bring together people from different groups into productive conversations where they could focus on a desirable future they had in common. There was no need to go through old battles or decide who was to blame. Everyone, from the leaders of CCMS to front line employees in far-flung regions, had a stake in it and could be personally committed to it. It was easy to call a meeting to discuss how to get more of it and have people volunteer to show up.

Table five shows a few other examples of adaptive challenges and related generative images.

Table 5 Examples of Generative Images

Adaptive Challenge	Future-focused, possibility-oriented purpose (Generative Image)
How do we integrate a newly acquired group of companies in the same business, so they don't act like regional fiefdoms and develop synergies and the ability to innovate at a global level	Be a truly *global* corporation
How do we increase the safety of miners who have resisted implementing new policies and procedures designed to increase safety because they feel they are too cumbersome and involve adding unnecessary work to their jobs?	Easy safety

How do we get the other departments in the organization to actively partner with the finance group in developing more adaptive, agile, financial controls?	Painless budgeting

Creating Generative Images

The purpose that is going to power a generative change has to combine the adaptive challenge the sponsor wants to manage with the inherent motivation of the stakeholders who will have to change. This can't be something just the sponsor or senior leaders care about. It's important to have a good sense of what the people you need to engage in the change process care about. In a smaller situation like this one, the leaders may have a good enough sense, especially if they have worked their way up to leadership positions. But the larger the group of stakeholders, the more likely the sponsors are not fully tuned into their real cares and concerns. This is one of the main reasons Dialogic OD efforts create design teams (other names for the same thing include steering groups and coordinating committees) that include people from the different stakeholder groups, forming a microcosm of the whole system you are trying to change. Hopefully, they will have a good sense of what all the stakeholders care about. They will have to identify the right purpose and if you are lucky, a good generative image.

I don't know of any formula for how to come up with a good generative image, and sometimes I've done a generative change project without one—but you still need a future-focused, possibility-oriented purpose statement. My and others' research shows that focusing people on what they want more of creates more generative conversations than focusing them on problems and what you don't want (Bushe & Paranjpey, 2014). But if you can come up with a good generative image, getting people engaged in generative conversations is usually easy.

For example, in this case "getting the right materials to the right place at the right time" was their purpose, and it could have been used in a generative change project. But it would have taken more effort to get the people on the warehouse floor and the regional stores to engage, because 1) there is nothing new about this conversation, it's what they've been focused on for years, 2) it's not that ambiguous—many people think they know what they need to do (it's because of other people or groups, or the system, that things don't always work). It looks more like a technical problem than an adaptive challenge, and 3) it isn't appealing —it's not inspiring, and it doesn't touch a real pain point the way "stress-free" did.

Combine Polarities

One of the easiest places to find a generative image is to combine two things that people have been treating as polarized and in an either/or way. In the case we've been following, managers thought if people followed the rules more often, they'd be less stressed, but they'd provide less customer service. By always giving their customers what they wanted, they created more of the anomalies that led people to yell at each other. Stress-free customer service was an example of taking an either/or and turning it into a both/and. Sustainable development, the most generative image of our time, did this as well. Before it showed up, people thought you could either look after the environment, or the economy, but not both. After 25 years sustainable development is still throwing off innovations, and still, no one can define what it is. If it were defined, it would stop being generative.

However, sustainable development is unusual in its ability to be generative in so many different contexts and cultures. Usually, an image is only generative in a specific context. There are lots of other organizations where stress-free customer service would not be generative because it would not be surprising, or ambiguous, or motivating or resolve a polarity. It isn't enough that the image is motivating—I've seen efforts to come up with generative images produce ideas that were more like marketing slogans. They were attractive, but they didn't focus people on the adaptive challenge, or they didn't capture anything people cared about. The generative image has to be focused on the real purpose—the underlying adaptive challenge, focused on what the sponsor wants people to be trying to do every day, framed to appeal to a latent or unexpressed common purpose.

How do you know if you have a good generative image? I don't have a formula for that either, but I can tell you that everyone knows it when they hear it. If you are working with a design team or leadership group, once a good generative image surfaces most people will recognize it. But not a bad idea to try it out on some of the different stakeholders you will want to engage in the change effort before you settle on it.

Checklist for Reframing the Adaptive Challenge

- ✓ Leaders are ready to try a generative change approach.
- ✓ You have identified the stakeholders who will need to change to manage the adaptive challenge.
- ✓ You have identified one or more polarities that are part of the organization's current stuckness.
- ✓ You are working with a group of people who have a good idea of what those stakeholders actually care about.
- ✓ Sponsors are clear about what they really care about.
- ✓ The people you will need to sponsor the generative change process are involved in reframing the adaptive challenge.
- ✓ You can reframe the adaptive challenge into something short and sweet that can be used to invite stakeholders into new conversations.

THREE

Engage Stakeholders in Generative Conversations

At the next Management Team (MT) meeting, the group discussed what they'd learned by testing out "stress-free customer service" as their purpose statement. Charlie concluded that in many ways, stress-free customer service was directly tied to material availability and that should be the focus of their work. They discussed many specific challenges different groups face with having the materials users needed, on hand. In some of the cases, the managers in the meeting had inaccurate perceptions about the actions of other groups related to those challenges. Robin pointed out that one of the "root storylines" (the same story keeps showing up in different ways) used to explain problems in material availability is something like "downstream thinks upstream takes its eyes off the ball; upstream thinks downstream is hiding/wasting/losing materials." Whenever a specific issue was looked at in-depth, however, the real reason was usually more reasonable. Robin noted that changing this storyline would be essential for real change to take hold.

The group circled back several times to issues around Regional Warehouses not knowing what is or isn't being delivered until a truck arrived. Much of the volatility in a keeper's ability to keep a month's supply of materials in stock could be related to this. The problems with the current software, and the amount of manual labor required for any proposed solution, resulted in no conclusions. It wasn't clear who was, or should be, the lead on ensuring keepers get advanced delivery notification.

At this point, Marty presented some analysis he had done on the nature and volume of materials they managed. While they had to look after over 5,000 different items, each with a separate catalog number, there were only about 250 that accounted for almost 70% of the volume of transactions they did. Those 250 were the bulk of what was regularly going through their system. The group got excited about engaging the organization in focusing on just those 250 items—what they decided to call High Volume Materials (HVM)—and work on making sure those are always in the right place at the right time. Charlie opined that whatever they developed to make that work could probably be spread to other materials later.

A few times a year all 14 supervisors and managers (see Figure 2 in Chapter 1) had a day-long meeting mainly filled with presentations and announcements. The next one was in a few weeks, and Robin described in general terms how an "engagement event" would work. People would be asked to identify the issues and then people invited to form small groups around the issues that most interested them, and encouraged to take the lead in creating solutions they would implement back at work. This garnered varying levels of support from the group. That way of doing things was very different from what people were used to, and members weren't sure it would be successful. They were concerned that people would hold back. A discussion ensued about the lack of trust people felt throughout the organization. A culture of "keep your head down and don't talk out of line" seemed widespread. Wally said, "you don't want to share your problems and you don't want to share your successes, because around here, if people hear you are having problems, they'll take away your headcount so someone else can manage them, or if they hear you are succeeding they'll say you don't need as many people. Either way, you lose". A lot of their front-line employees had seen change programs come and go; there was bound to be some cynicism. But, since Charlie seemed committed, they put their best effort in to make it successful. They wanted to make sure that some time was spent initially explaining the process. In the spirit of "those who will have to implement the change should be invited to the conversation", the group agreed to invite unionized crew leads from each of the units to the meeting, unsure how many would come, as this, again, was very unusual. Charlie decided to make up to 2-3 more spots available to all the different areas, and the first people to step forward would be invited, with their expenses paid.

Ester: I guess we should hold back and not participate to encourage others to step in?

Robin: I think your desire to engage others is a good thing, but you should participate just like everyone else. Don't dominate conversations, but follow your energy and get involved in those ideas that excite you.

    Look, guys, I know right now it seems like running a meeting this way is risky, but you are going to find out that there will be lots of energy and that holding the event is the easy part. Where your leadership is going to be crucial is after the event. But this is a very different kind of leadership from what you are used to.

    We don't want to use the event to have people make proposals, then decide which ones' you support and turn them into projects to manage. Instead, we want to use the meeting to have people with similar ideas and motivations find each other, propose changes they're personally committed to, and encourage everyone who has an idea that meets your guidelines just to go make it happen. You are not there to pick winners; we are there to launch as many experiments as possible and then learn as we go.

    People have to believe that these are real experiments and they won't be held responsible for being successful. Otherwise, people will be much more hesitant to try something new. Any experiment that meets the guidelines should be welcomed with the understanding that it's OK to fail because we'll learn something from it.

    After the meeting is when your leadership becomes critical. You have to pay close attention and find ways to monitor what is happening as a result of the event, and then lead in ways that support and amplify successful changes. You need to keep the momentum up, advertise and celebrate successes. Learn from the failures and celebrate those too.

Charlie: This is really going to be different, but I'm excited by it. If it works, it could improve everything we do. But I don't think calling them "experiments" will go over well in our culture. How about "pilot projects"? That is something people are used to.

Robin: That's great. Pilot projects it is. How are you going to be able to stay on top of whatever pilots get started?

The group discussed some options and decided on choosing one "tracker". Brenda was one of their peers who had been put on a special project. She had been replaced by Marty, but that project was delayed, so Brenda was back working for Charlie. They made it Brenda's job to stay in touch with all the pilots and create a continuous feedback loop so that the managers, and the rest of CCMS, knew what was happening. Since they only had two weeks before the meeting, it was decided to forgo any steering committee and leave it up to Charlie and Robin to design the meeting and to describe Brenda's role to her.

The Design of the First Engagement Event

The event took place from 10 to 4 on a Thursday in a very large room in a training facility. Initially, in one corner of the room, chairs were lined up, theatre-style facing a screen. In the other three corners, spaces for O&S, CW, and RW were identified, with flip charts, markers, and tape, so that they had as much separation from each other as possible.

In addition to the 14 managers and supervisors shown in Figure 1, about 25 unionized crew leads from all over CCMS had volunteered to discuss how to create stress-free customer service. Charlie started the meeting by introducing Brenda and Robin and their roles, and then laid out the objectives for the day:

1. Develop solutions that will enable the stress-free, reliable supply of high volume materials to our customers.

2. Improve cross-functional collaboration across CCMS

Charlie described his view of CCMS and what he wanted to do to create an organization able to provide stress-free customer service. He described why they had chosen HVM as the initial focus for change and then invited Marty to describe what HVM were. Marty did a 10-minute presentation on his analysis of HVM, and then the floor was opened to questions for Charlie or Marty. There weren't many.

Robin did a short presentation on why generative change rather than the usual approach. During this, he described how people in organizations make up stories about what is going on in other groups to explain things to themselves but don't usually check those stories out, and how this creates barriers and mistrust[4]. Robin offered the root storyline he had picked up about upstream and downstream as an example and said what they were to do in the morning was to check out stories, and understand what goes on outside their own areas. Robin emphasized that the only way things can get better is if people are willing to describe their needs and put them on the table.

> Robin: The first rule of building collaboration in organizations is you have to ask for what you want.

Someone in the group: "I want a raise." (general laughter)

> Robin: And the second rule is don't expect to get it. Just because you want something doesn't mean it's anyone else's mission to give it to you, but at least they'll know what you want so there's a much better chance you might get it.

Another voice in the group: "Like what happens with my wife." (more laughter)

Robin then did a quick description of the generative change process and described how the afternoon would revolve around whatever they personally wanted to work on. He then outlined the principles the Management Team had articulated for this and future engagement events.

- Every event has a specific issue to work on (not an opportunity to raise other issues).
- As much as possible, the people who will have to make any solutions work are invited to the event.
- Participating in an event is voluntary.
- During the event, people with ideas and energy propose pilot projects to deal with the issue.
- Any pilot that meets the guidelines is welcome (the guidelines will be gone over later).
- After the event, everyone is encouraged to do what they can to make their pilots successful.
- Management's role is to monitor and report on pilot progress and look for ways to build on and embed successful pilots.

---

4 This problem, and solutions to it, are discussed in G. Bushe (2009)

- Pilots are useful for testing new ideas and concepts, and it is expected that people proposing a pilot give it some effort. It is not expected that every pilot will be successful; however, those that do not succeed will provide opportunities for useful learning.

An agenda that outlined the design for the day was distributed, (See Table 6) and the rest of the day pretty much followed it. First, the three groups were asked to meet separately and prepare a presentation on "What about HV Materials causes us stress." During each presentation, others were encouraged to ask questions to understand the other units' issues. Then the three groups met separately again, this time to prepare two lists for each of the other two groups: 1) How you could reduce stress for us and 2) How we think we could reduce stress for you. These lists were again presented to the whole group and questions encouraged. Then each group quickly huddled and decided which members would meet with the other two groups. While this was happening, the corners were changed from group areas to inter-group areas (e.g. CW & RW). All the lists relevant to that pairing were put up on the wall in that corner. People were told to meet in those corners and discuss ideas for supporting stress-free customer service. If some people wanted to break off and form a smaller group to work on an idea, that was fine. People were introduced to the "law of two feet"[5]—if you aren't contributing or interested in what's happening, go somewhere else. In the last 40 minutes, the group reassembled and anyone who had a pilot proposal described it, the group that was involved in it and identified who the "champion" for the team was. Charlie emphasized that people should "just go do it" and that Brenda would stay in touch with everyone.

Table 6: The Design of the first CCMS Engagement Event

30 mins	Each of the three units (O&S, CW, & RW) meet to answer the question; "What about HV materials causes us stress." They brainstorm a list on flipchart paper and pick a spokesperson (other than the manager) to present that to the rest of the group

---

5 A key idea from Open Space Technology

30 mins	Presentations are made, and after each presentation, people ask questions	
45 mins	Each of the units meets again to discuss what they've just heard from the other two groups and make two lists for each of the two other groups: How you could reduce HVM related stress for us How we think we could reduce HVM related stress for you Again, these are listed on flipcharts and a spokesperson chosen This activity will bleed into lunch so that groups that are finished can eat while unfinished groups can keep working and perhaps eat while in discussions.	
60 mins	Lunch—a buffet lunch is brought into the room for people to eat when they want	
45 mins	Presentations are made, with Q&A encouraged at any point in a presentation	
15 mins	Each unit meets again to discuss what they have heard. They decide how best to split up to meet with representatives of the other two groups to discuss ideas for reducing HVM related stress they are causing each other. Three corners of the room are changed from areas for a specific unit, to areas for pairs of units. The flip charts of wants and offers for each pairing are put up in their respective spaces	

15 mins	Charlie does a presentation on the guidelines for pilot projects.
	• Not too complicated
	• Reduces, or does not increase, anyone's stress
	• Won't increase Consolidated's net costs or increase headcount
	• Uses (or doesn't circumvent) the IT system
	• Supports CCMS's ability to adjust to the unexpected
	• Improves (or doesn't diminish) relationships between all parts of the supply chain
	He emphasizes that subgroups can break away to work on specific ideas—they don't have to all stay together
60 mins	Three inter-groups meet to come up with pilot projects for improving stress-free customer service of HVM. Only pilots one or more people are willing to "champion" are to be presented
30 mins	Pilots are presented to the whole group. Volunteer "leads" for each pilot are identified.
30 mins	Charlie fields any final questions. People are encouraged to go do it.

—Pause in the story—

Designing Generative Conversations

Most Dialogic OD methods[6] are different ways to design generative conversations, and I won't spend time here going over them. You can find many of them briefly described in The Change Handbook (Holman, Devane & Cady, 2007) and expand your repertoire from there. Learning these different methods is very useful as it offers you a wide array of tools for your tool belt—but using them in a simple "paint by numbers" way will lead to inconsistent results. Dialogic Organization Develop-

---

6 Got to b-m-insitute.com for a constantly updated bibliography of Dialogic OD methods.

ment is a theory base for how to use any method that will lead to more consistently successful change. You want to be able to mix and match different methods with the best chance of achieving the desired outcomes with this group, at this time, in this place with the opportunities and constraints it faces. The chapter by Jacob Storch (2015) describes how to design generative conversations in some detail.

When using a generative change process, I tell my clients "the ideal is to close down the whole organization and put everyone in the same room for a couple of days. If we can't do that, let's work back from that to what we can do." I look for ways to work with the natural ebb and flow of this organization's life. In the case, CCMS had a quarterly meeting with a lot of the key stakeholders coming up, so it was fairly easy to build on that and reformat the meeting to create generative conversations. The design started with a variation on an intergroup mirror exercise (Blake, Shepard & Mouton, 1964) followed with a kind of structured open space.

One of my mantras is "whoever will need to change needs to be invited to the conversation." It doesn't mean they have to show up, but a fundamental assumption about generative change is that more change happens more quickly the more stakeholders are involved in the same engagement events. If people are forced to show up, however, you don't know if they are interested in or engaged by the purpose. The worst-case scenario is that they are opposed to the purpose and work to sabotage the event. Making attendance at engagement events voluntary makes it more likely that everyone there is predisposed to contribute positively. In many organizations, there will be a group of people who are not interested in getting engaged. People's interest will depend on many things, like the amount of cynicism in the organization, how many years they have left before retirement, how compelling the purpose is. Not everyone has to engage for generative change to happen. Work with the willing and trust in the power of the grapevine. If people have a positive experience, word will get out, and interest in engaging will grow.

In the case, while managers and supervisors were told that attendance was voluntary, the expectation that the group of 14 would meet every quarter was very strong. No one chose not to come, and it was clear that there were a few who didn't engage with the process. This is a danger you face when engagement events are interlaced with regular events. Fortunately, in this case, that wasn't disruptive.

On the other hand, it is often the case that some key people or groups need to be part of the event for it to be successful. Think of people with control over key resources. People who control organizational processes. People whose opposition to an idea could kill it. The last thing you want to do is hold an engagement event that gets people excited and builds momentum for change and then gets killed by some authority who doesn't understand what is going on or doesn't support it. Think about the purpose you are trying to accomplish, the stakeholders who are key to accomplishing it, and the kinds of changes they are likely to propose. Now think about who else will have to support those changes—those people need to not only be invited to the event; they need to have the generative change process explained to them as well as why they are so critical to its success. Hopefully, the purpose will be of interest to them as well, and the event can be scheduled so they can attend. In this case, Robin checked that out early on by questioning the MT about who else outside CCMS, including Charlie's boss, had important interdependencies with CCMS that needed to be considered in designing an engagement event. As it turned out, CCMS was pretty independent and could make changes internally without needing the consent of others. In other cases, however, when an outside group has to be part of the process, you will need to take the time to ensure that the right person from that group is co-sponsoring the event, or someone higher up that both groups ultimately report to is a sponsor. You have to ensure that s/he understands the generative change model, and signs off on the purpose and design of the process.

A key to increasing the creativity and innovation that emerges from engagement events is increasing the diversity of participants. Innovation often comes from the margins of organizations, among those who have not had much voice or ability to influence the organization. It is through different perspectives rubbing up against each other that new ideas are born. Open Space Technology, in which participants design the entire content of the event during the event, can be incredibly transformational or produce very little and this seems to depend on the amount of "heat" in the room—the more heat, the more transformation. Harrison Owen (2008) has identified the following ingredients as necessary for successful Open Space: a purpose people care about, conflict, passion, urgency, diversity of views and voluntary presence. When there is a lot of energy and desire for change amongst the group of stakeholders, you don't need a lot of design. When there is less urgency or passion, some structure helps. But in all cases, you need different perspectives in the mix to produce something new, and people who care enough about it to mix it up.

Building the Three Enablers of Transformational Change into Engagement Events

In design and hosting, you need to think about what is going to result in productive change. Marshak and I have shown that successful Dialogic OD doesn't happen unless one of three things happen (Bushe & Marshak, 2014)

A generative image captures the right stakeholders' attention and catalyzes new thoughts and conversations

We looked at generative images, in-depth, in Chapter 2. In the case, stress-free customer service was a good generative image. It was a purpose everyone could embrace, for themselves and for others. It was appealing, and since no one knew, practically, how to do that, they were motivated to work together to figure it out. Over the next 18 months, storekeepers and warehouse employees became actively engaged in all manner of transforming shipping and receiving. A "working together to accomplish our purpose" ethos emerged that was evident, top to bottom.

The current way things are is disrupted, and people are encouraged to self-organize in pursuit of the purpose to find a better way

Disruption is often necessary for transformational change to occur. This can be difficult for many managers as maintaining stability and predictable performance is often their job. Disruption can look like failure. Just the word disruption evokes images of pressure, hard feelings, conflict—which can be true but doesn't have to be. Inspiration can be disruptive too. I think one of the reasons for the success of appreciative inquiry is that focusing on what works and on strengths is very disruptive in an organization that habitually focuses on what isn't working and problems. Disruption in a system where people aren't happy doesn't feel bad if it creates hope.

One of the theoretical foundations of Dialogic OD is complexity science and what we have learned about the self-organizing nature of systems, and what we have learned about emergence—the way nature changes (Holman, 2010). What I have found is that people are always self-organizing, but without the right things in place, they will mostly self-organize to protect their own interests and the interests of groups they identify with. If you bring people from different groups into the same room and only disrupt how they normally interact, they are most likely to re-organize in a way that is fragmented, protecting or advancing the interests and agendas of their own groups. People, however, even if they are from different groups, will self-organize in the service of the whole IF they truly share a common purpose. Organizing generative conversations around a purpose that everyone in the conversation cares about is critical for a generative change process to work.

In the case, hearing about life in the other parts of the organization was disruptive and opened up channels for energy and communication. Just discussing in their groups, how others could reduce stress for them and, especially, how they could reduce stress for others, was disruptive—the latter wasn't something they had talked about before. Notice the question was framed to focus on what the management team wanted more of (how we can reduce stress for each other). They could also have constructed a similar exercise asking each group to describe "how we create stress for each other". That would be a common "diagnostic" move in planned change efforts, but there is some evidence that focusing on what you don't want reduces generativity, leading to fewer ideas, less richness in thinking and conversations and less energy to act on new ideas (Bushe & Paranjpey, 2014). Sometimes it may be appropriate to focus a group on what's wrong, what's not working and why, but you want to have time to refocus them on what they want in the future in order to power the next step in generative change: launching self-initiated probes.

A core narrative about the way things are is changed

Every organization has "narratives", storylines about the way things are, and why things happen the way they do. Each of us has narratives about ourselves and others that we use to make sense of what is happening around us. People in organizations use shared root storylines to make sense of the decisions and actions of their leaders. For example, whether employees see a new outsourcing initiative as a smart move to support their success, or a threat to jobs, will depend on the narrative they have about their leaders' intentions. That is why trying to copy an innovation that worked in company A into company B rarely produces the same results. It's also one of the reasons generative change produces more change than planned change—it works with narrative processes rather than battling against them. There is evidence that planned change efforts rarely work unless leaders recognize and work to alter core narratives at the same time (Hastings & Schwartz, 2019).

By framing expectations, narratives are a powerful stabilizing force in social life. We see what we believe, and our actions are shaped by how we think the future will unfold. Changing how people show up at work often requires changing their beliefs about how things are around here. In an organization where "managers decide and workers do as told", creating a more engaged, adaptive workforce will require changing that narrative. You don't change narratives by declaring what the new narrative ought to be; you change narratives by acting differently.

In the case, at the end of the first engagement event, the beginning of a change of core narrative could be detected (which you will see more of in the next chapters). Misperceptions were changed, and a greater sense of personal responsibility for personal and organizational success was kindled. But there was also a lot of wait and see—totally justified caution about whether the invitation for supervisors and workers to take charge of their ideas would really be supported. As you will see, it was. The MT built on success, learned from failures, and developed a more agile, adaptive organization. Narratives of cynicism were replaced with narratives of hope, and then narratives of pride.

Hosting, not Facilitating

A facilitator is someone who helps a group of people work together effectively by guiding conversations, asking questions, helping spread participation, capturing ideas, suggesting processes for group work and then leading them. Normally, they don't have a personal interest in the issues being discussed, so they can guide interactions to produce outcomes the entire group is satisfied with.

However, some question whether this kind of facilitating produces less generative conversations (Goppelt & Ray, 2015; Zubizarreta, 2014). When a consultant stands at the front of the group, capturing what people are saying on a board, all eyes are on him or her. That is not a conversation among stakeholders, that is a conversation where stakeholders are feeding the consultant what they think they are being asked for. Often, the outputs are clichéd, easy to justify, and abstract. While they might look like a great list, they rarely power any change in behavior. I am now of the opinion that if the people in the room are talking to me (the consultant) instead of to each other, something's wrong.

Hosting has become a commonly used metaphor to describe a different approach to leading meetings (McKergow & Bailey, 2014). This is often described as creating "containers" that support people having new and better conversations (Bushe, 2010; Corrigan, 2015). Typically, these are not facilitated. One reason is that it would require a small army of facilitators if you are working with a large group. Instead, design engagement events so that small groups can work on their own (Weisbord & Janoff, 2007). How much structure will be required depends on the group, its size, and how familiar or foreign the tasks they will be asked to do. It's not unusual to compose a workbook that describes to participants what each step in the day is, provides cues and questions for small group discussions, and so on. Overall, generative conversations need to be designed to step people through a sequence of activities where the following will happen

1. Do people know why they are here? If not, design a process to make that happen.

2. Are people willing to say what they really think, feel and want? If not, design a process that will make it more likely that people will. Issues of safety are the most important here. Does this group have a history of distrust, and if so, how will that be managed?

3. Do people know what they need to know to come up with practical new ideas and innovations? If not, design a process that will help them discover what they need to know.

4. Good hosting requires paying attention to the energy and being ready to redesign on the fly when unexpected things show up (Bushe, 2010). To produce probes, however, the design will have

to be sequenced so that it naturally leads to people self-selecting themselves into groups focused on something they want to do.

Checklist for Hosting Generative Conversations

- ✓ You have a clear purpose people care about, and have identified what is in bounds and what is out of bounds.
- ✓ You have the right space for people to be able to move around, as needed.
- ✓ The key sponsor(s) will be there at the beginning to explain the purpose and process and answer questions, and there at the end to hear and bless probes. If they can be there for the entire event, even better.
- ✓ Your design will ensure that people know why they are there, can say what they think, and will get whatever information they need to come up with practical ideas.
- ✓ You have provided just the right amount of structure so people have a sense of the beginning, middle and end of the event, and can step into productive conversations they want to be having.
- ✓ You create opportunities for the large group to check in on what is happening without long, laborious "report outs".
- ✓ Your design helps people who don't know each other very well uncover who has similar interests, motivations, and ideas and lets them team up to create a probe.
- ✓ There is some way of supporting/amplifying people's commitment to acting on their ideas.

FOUR

Launch Self-Initiated Probes and Learn as You Go

A week after the engagement event, the MT met along with Brenda and Robin. The mood was exuberant.

Charlie That was awesome! I couldn't believe how much energy was in that room.

Marty Yeah. And the buzz has already started. The next day I had people in the O&S office telling me they regret not having come and asked me when they would get to attend an event.

Ester It was great to see people from different groups working together all over the room. It was sort of chaotic but not really. You could see some guys hanging back at first, but as the day went on people moved to the groups they wanted to be a part of. I thought just about everyone was fully engaged.

Charlie Thirteen pilots!! I didn't think it would be that good.

Wally Yeah, by the end I was having trouble keeping track of all the stuff that was going on.

Robin And that's one of the reasons we need a tracker. Brenda, were you able to get a list of all the pilots with champions?

Brenda passes out the list of pilots and describes her plan to contact all the leads in the next week and get some idea of what their strategy is and what they are planning to do next.

Charlie Did any of you see what was going on in the corner with Betty, Alice, Mo, and Harb? Turns out we haven't been updating the standard package sizes vendors ship parts to us

	in our catalog, so keepers put in an order for, say, 125 bolts because they think that's how it comes, but they now actually come in boxes of 120. So then a guy in the warehouse gets the order and has to open another box to take out 5 to put in the box that's going to be shipped.
Ester	Yah, and then puts the box back on the shelf that now only has 115.
Charlie	Yeah, and the keeper didn't need 125, he just ordered that size thinking that was the standard package.
Brenda	Since she started looking into it Friday morning, Betty's discovered that more than half of the items she's checked are coming in different amounts than what's in the catalog. After she's done with HVM she's going to go over everything else.
Marty	Ohh, that's what Betty was on such a tear about in the office Friday.
Ester	That one change alone is going to make a huge difference to order accuracy and to the time it takes to pick an order.
Wally	That's great, but I'm not sure how some of the other pilots are going to work. I could see at the end of the day some people were pretty confused about what was going to happen next. They just aren't used to being told to go do it, and anyway, it's unclear how they should go about working on things.

This leads to a conversation about how engagement events need a better way to end. The group decides at the next one to create a "coaches' corner" of all the MT members. Groups who want to champion a pilot would each meet with the MT, describe their plans and get some coaching. The group thought this would create more certainty, help with the launch and commitment process, and help the MT better understand and support the pilots.

Ester	Some of the pilots are things people can work on their own, like standard packaging, but some are pretty big issues.
Wally	It was great to be in that room, and I think people were sincere in their participation, but I worry that the bloom will fade and not much will happen if we don't step in and hold people accountable.
Robin	I think your concerns about not losing momentum are extremely valid, and one of our big challenges is how to

	track and support the pilots, nurture the good ideas and embed them into the daily operations. But I'm afraid that if you turn them into projects, where people are held accountable to deliver on promises, you will kill the energy and goodwill you built last week. This is important—when you meet with people working on pilots the tone has to NOT be "you here to report to management and we will tell you what to do next." The tone has to be like a group of allies, sitting around the fire, discussing how the battle is going and planning their next move.
Marty	If we don't supervise what people are doing, how do we keep up the momentum?
Charlie	We already have some quick wins to publicize. In addition to standard packaging, Andy has been able to create a huge turnaround with our problem contractor. They were actually really happy that we offered to go and teach them how to interface with our systems. Andy's been there twice and was able to get them to stop putting in 6 months' worth of inventory in one order and pare it back to a few weeks at a time.
Marty	That's huge for keeping our supply fluctuations down.

This leads to a discussion of how to go about celebrating "wins" and using that to maintain momentum. They discuss how to inform the rest of CCMS about what is going on, and how to keep up regular communications. The group agrees a "culture of celebration" does not exist in Consolidated Construction and it will take some effort to change.

Wally	What we want to avoid is our history of starting things and not completing. We should pare down the list and focus people on what can be accomplished.
Robin	The idea in generative change is that you allow what works to work and what doesn't, doesn't. Good ideas will attract support—people will self-organize around them. Bad ideas won't.
Charlie	I don't think we want to tell someone who has signed up to champion a pilot that we now don't want them to do it, but I also think we need to make sure people have what they need to be successful.

Robin   Exactly, that's why we need the tracker to keep us in the loop about what's happening and what people need to move forward.

Ester   Yeah, but, one day turn around on HVM orders?!?

Charlie   I couldn't believe Cady, of all people, agreed to take that on.

At this point, a long discussion takes place over whether there is any chance of reducing the current three-day turnaround, from the time an order is placed by a keeper, to the time it is put on a truck out of Central Warehouse, to one day. Various theories for why Mike Cady, a grizzled 40 year veteran of CCMS, with a fairly cynical demeanor, had even proposed such a pilot are kicked around. They range from an attempt to show that the emergent change process is a load of manure, to the notion that he embraced the idea of a pilot as an opportunity to learn without needing to succeed. Debate revolves around whether to take the pilot seriously and put resources behind it or to ignore it and let it quietly fade away.

Marty   What happens in this company is that we get fixated on a number and then the debate is all around the number. We may not be able to reduce turnaround to 24 hours, but we sure can reduce turnaround time.

Robin   What I think Mike was responding to, and you know his buddy Joe Clinge was a big part of that group's conversation, is that keepers have to make their next order before they know if they are getting everything from their last order. It ends up creating a lot of stress for the keepers, and people find various ways to game the system.

A conversation breaks out about the different reasons why orders aren't filled and how the current IT system deals with them and why that creates confusion and stress for keepers. The group agrees there is no practical way to fix the problem manually, and no way to get resources to fix an IT system that is slated to be replaced, though it is unclear when.

Charlie   The thing is, if you look at this list (of pilots) there are four that require heavy lifting. They aren't things anyone can change on their own:
- Backorder process

- 24-hour turnaround
- HVM order schedule
- Accurate orders out on time

Ester   Yeah, and they're all interrelated.
Wally   And no one can fix those things by themselves.
Robin   I agree. I'm wondering if this is worth having another engagement event?
Charlie   Totally!

The group identifies several relationships between accuracy, on-time delivery, and the "backorder" issue embedded in each of those four pilots. They decide to invite everyone who had championed the four pilots to be on a team to design another engagement event. They delegate Charlie, Ester, and Robin to organize that and get the event done in the next 30 days. Most of the changes will be required of people at Central Warehouse, but the group discusses who else should be involved in the event. They discuss relationships with other groups at Consolidated that could impact any solutions and how best to communicate and work with them. They decide to identify the groups inside and outside Material Supply that could play a part in any solutions and make attendance voluntary. That would ensure only people with energy and motivation attend.

When Robin next met with Charlie and Ester, he suggested they find a better phrase than "engagement event", which he thought was too generic and didn't have any juice to it. That started a conversation that lasted a few weeks, and what the MT and Design Team finally decided on was "crewshop". That became a very potent symbol of the changing narrative at CCMS and was commonly used as both a noun (let's have a crewshop) and a verb (we need to crewshop that).

With Robin's facilitation, the Design Team started their first meeting by creating a common map of how the system is supposed to work. They created a flow chart of the various activities and groups that impact timely and accurate materials delivery (See Figure 4). They decided that there were four semi-independent chunks in the process, and different groups had more or less to do with each one. It seemed to make more sense to run different engagement events that would target these different parts of the process.

1. Field Ordering and Pick Scheduling: how do we ensure accurate, consistent, on-time ordering and clear scheduling of HVM delivery?
2. Outbound and Field Receipt: How do we ensure accurate, on-time shipping and receipt of HVM?
3. Inbound: How do we ensure accurate, fast, visible replenishment?

In parallel, and then again after we have dealt with the three above

4. Backorder visibility: what are the different kinds of backorders? How do we ensure everyone knows why they happened, when they will be filled, and what people have to do?

They thought it best to spend a whole day in a crewshop focused on #1 with representatives from the warehouse and field stores. Take what was learned from day one and spend the morning of the next day on #2, with everyone from Outbound operations in the Central Warehouse, along with representatives from other groups. The afternoon, work on #3 (Inbound), incorporating what had emerged from the previous two crewshops. Involve everyone in Inbound operations, but again with representatives of the other groups. People from the other groups would be invited to volunteer to attend the meeting. How this would affect operations would be sorted out depending on how many volunteered.

At the second Design Team meeting, the purpose of **ensuring Field Stores get their HVM orders before they have to place their next order** seemed to capture something all the stakeholders cared about. They decided that the sessions focused on the warehouse should take place in the warehouse, where people could prototype and design solutions at the site itself. Nothing like that had ever been done before, so Robin and Ester later walked around the warehouse and figured out a way space could be organized to bring everyone together and to be able to meet in small groups.

To speed up the crewshops, particularly the half-day ones, the group decided to identify the most likely issues people would want to work on so they didn't have to spend time during the crewshop identifying issues. People would have a chance to add to them if they wanted.

For the first crewshop, Charlie invited all the regional managers and the first six keepers to volunteer, as well as some spaces for anyone who

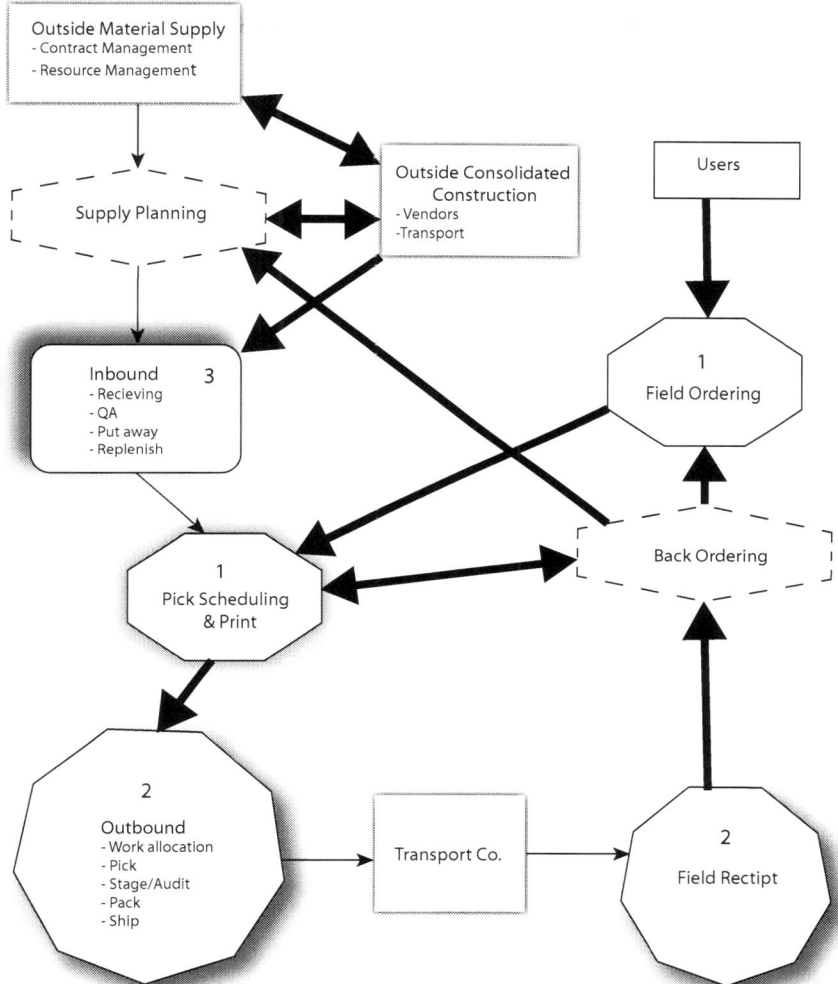

Figure 4. CCMS workflow with crewshop groupings identified (dark arrows signify process challenges)

worked at Central Warehouse and wanted to attend. Managers and supervisors in pick scheduling were invited, along with the first five employees in that area to volunteer. The supervisors of Inbound and Outbound, two from procurement, and the whole management team were included. It was held at a large meeting room in a Consolidated building close to the Central Warehouse.

Table 7. Design of the HVM Turnaround, First Day Crewshop

9:00	5 mins	Opening Welcoming—Charlie—the purpose of the day
	10 mins	HVM story—Charlie explains the discussions that have taken place at the MT and why they have chosen HVM. He shows the data on which materials are the bulk of what they process.
	10 mins	Results from the last engagement session. Reports from pilots in progress/completed—Charlie
9:30	15mins	Limitations of the current system's capabilities—Marty & Brenda discuss the problems and limitations of their current IT system and while there are plans for significant change, it won't happen for a couple of years.
	10 mins	Principles of Crewshops and overview to the day—Robin explains the idea of working across boundaries, at the front lines, to identify problems and for groups with an idea and energy to pursue it, to do so. He says that every idea generated here will be allowed to prove itself, and they will all be regarded as pilots. He emphasizes the need for focus on the purpose of this crewshop, and describes how to use the parking lot for side issues.
10:00	10 mins	Ester describes the issues that are available to work on and asks if any are missing. No one offers any. She then invites people to go to the issue they want to work on and identify the 1-3 problems that need solutions—not to come up with solutions but to describe the problem as clearly as possible.

	40 mins	Each issue is on a separate piece of flip chart paper, taped to the wall, spaced around the room. People go to the one they want to work on. A few get large crowds. A couple get no one at all. Their task is to arrive at a shared definition of the problem. The pre-defined issues are: Prioritizing orders Smoothing demand Order-transport schedule Backorder handling Placing HVM orders Standard package ordering Material requisition approval
11:00	20 mins	Report out problem statements. Look for overlaps and consolidate. Develop a single set of problem statements.
	5 mins	Criteria for Solutions—Charlie goes over the guidelines for pilots • Doesn't increase headcount • Leverages the systems we have • Continue to meet other customer needs • Reduces stress or doesn't increase anyone's stress
11:30	75 mins	Robin explains the pilot project process and that groups can sub-group and the "law of two feet". He explains that groups can work through lunch and to work toward a proposal by 1:30, giving themselves 30-45 mins for lunch. People go to the problem statement they want to work on developing solutions.
12:30ish	45 mins	LUNCH—buffet style so people can have it when they want it.

1:30	45 mins	Proposals are written up on flip charts. Everyone mills about reading them and comments on what they like and concerns or suggestions with post-it notes
2:15	60–90 mins	Groups consider the feedback and have a second round on refining proposals and planning action steps
3:00	60 mins	The coaches' corner opens. When groups are ready, they come and describe their pilot, describe what they need and get advice.
4:00		Close

Six pilots emerge; two depend on what happens at later crewshops.

The next morning the Outbound operations at the Central Warehouse are stopped while all personnel, regional managers plus some regional and Inbound reps, crowd into the one meeting room above the warehouse floor. Regional supervisors explain the stress created by having to put in their weekly order before knowing what they will get from their last order. The complexity of the information and systems problem is uncovered, and the stress created for everyone else from "the backorder problem" is acknowledged. Mike Cady, the Outbound supervisor who championed 24-hour turnaround makes a pitch for why he thinks one-day turnaround on HVM is doable and would reduce everyone's stress. After, they all go to a large, empty tunnel area with signs on the wall for the pre-identified issues. People go to the issue they want to work on and teams form.

Table 8. Design of the HVM Turnaround Second Day Morning (Outbound)

8:00	5 mins	Opening Welcoming—Charlie—the purpose of the day
	10 mins	HVM story—Charlie
	10 mins	Results from last month's first crewshop. Report outs on pilots in progress/completed—Charlie

	15 mins	Results from yesterday. Pilots that may affect today's actions—Ester
8:40	10 mins	Principles of Crewshops and overview to the morning—Robin
	15 mins	Why this purpose—Regional Managers and Mike Cady
	10 mins	List of issues—Ester
	5 mins	Explain the pilot project process. Criteria for Solutions—Ester • Doesn't increase headcount • Leverages the systems we have • Continue to meet other customer needs • Reduces stress or doesn't increase anyone's stress
9:30	60 mins	People go to the issue statement they want to work on developing solutions for. Explain that groups can sub-group and the law of two feet. Prepare to present proposals. Of the eight issues, only five get interest: • Identify and stage HVM • Ensure HVM pick accuracy • Pack to make it easy for keeper put-away • Communicate physical stock-outs to keepers when picks are completed • Collapse HVM picks from 3 days to 1 with current resources
10:30	30 mins	Each group presents proposals. People write down feedback as they listen, which is collected and given back to each group.
11:00	20-50 mins	Groups regroup to consider feedback, refine pilot projects and plan next steps

11:15	45 mins	Coaches' corner opens
12:00		Close

The energy in the Warehouse goes through the roof as squads of employees roam about looking at how they can redesign all aspects of operations to get 24-hour turnaround of HV materials. Managers can't believe the full engagement of what had appeared to be an apathetic, cynical workforce. Six high-quality pilots emerge, only one of which is dependent on others for success. A pizza lunch is served for all, and Inbound personnel saunter over to partake and can feel the positive energy in the air.

The afternoon starts quickly with full engagement as the other side of the warehouse feels a little competitive to be even more amazing.

Table 9 Design of the HVM Turnaround Second Day Afternoon (Inbound)

12:30	5 mins	Opening Welcoming—Charlie—the purpose of the day
	10 mins	HVM story—Charlie
	10 mins	Results from last month's first crewshop. Report outs on pilots in progress/completed— Charlie
	10 mins	Results from yesterday and this morning. Pilots that may affect today's actions—Ester
	10 mins	Principles of Crewshops and overview to the afternoon—Robin
	15mins	Best practices for warehouses—Marty
1:30	5 mins	Explain the pilot project process. Criteria for Solutions—Ester
	25 mins	People go to one of the two general areas they want to work on: receiving materials or putting away materials. Each group identifies issues and prioritizes them.

2:00	20 mins	Each group presents issues and priorities; a large group discussion follows. Areas of overlap between the two groups' lists are identified and they produce a single set of issues.
3:00	30-45 mins	People invited to the issue they want to work on and develop pilots
3:15	45 mins	Coaches' corner opens
4:00		Close

Five pilots emerge. In all, 17 pilots have emerged, and there is real commitment to 1-day turnaround of HV materials.

For the next few days, there is a bit of a giddy euphoria among the Management Team and among some employees. Everyone seems impressed by what happened. Mike Cady, the Central Warehouse supervisor who surprised managers when he championed 1-day turnaround, tells whoever will listen, "this is the way to manage."

One week later Ester broadcast the following email to all of CCMS

Hello all,

I wanted to reach out and communicate the work that has been undertaken to create "stress-free customer service" within our operations. All told, the four Crewshop sessions generated (19) unique pilot projects…..quite a big piece of work!

Just to recap on what has brought us to this point—since our first Crewshop over a month ago, about 100 different people from all over Material Supply have participated at some point in coming up with ideas for how we can ensure that HVM materials are always in the right place at the right time. People at all levels have stepped forward to champion pilot projects they think will make a difference. This consolidated list of HVM pilots is attached, and also the Intranet site we have created for tracking progress on the pilots, below. As you can see below…you all have been quite busy working on making these pilots projects a reality.

Earlier this week Brenda and I re-connected with those of you who had taken the lead on some of the Outbound or Inbound "HVM

Crewshop" pilots to get a sense of what progress had been made so far, and what was next for these pilot projects.

So far, in the past week:

Vera Sarcovic, Betty Chan, Gerry Gunster, Charlie Green, Val McKenzie, and the *Inbound Operations teams* have made significant headway on correcting "Standard Pack" quantities in the catalog, with only (35) more Catalog ID's remaining to be corrected. This will simplify receiving of HVM materials, and should align standard pack quantities with Field HVM order quantities;

Andy Shore has led the revisions to the Fields' "HVM Order Form", making it easier to place HVM orders by formatting the order form and using simple Excel functions;

Dave Piller, Bob Sun, Buddy Long and Mike Cady have ordered (52) returnable Plastipack shipping containers and "HVM Order" labels, to be used during an HVM pilot project in the Lower Mainland. These should arrive in a week or so;

Outbound Operations has dedicated resources to the HVM picks at the Central Distribution Centre, and validated outgoing a sampling of HVM picks for accuracy and presentation;

Patti Bruce, Lyn Kowalski, Larry Levesque, Raj Singh, and *Alice Mills* have made progress on piloting weekly HVM shipments to the Skeena region, vs. bi-weekly;

Phil Reimer and *Brenda Sawchuk* have started communicating to Field end what Catalog ID's are physically stocked out at Central Warehouse, before the materials ship;

John Stoltz, Andre Lacouer and *Ivan Riksman* have dedicated an area of the Receiving floor for only HVM materials, and are utilizing mobile carts to receive HVM orders—ensuring HVM orders are received on a daily basis;

 Hal Baumer and *Alice Mills* have started discussions with QA on how to expedite QA processing of received materials.

. . . that's amazing progress to make in only a week- all credit to the hard work and dedication you've demonstrated in seeing these pilots progress.

And if I've missed mentioning something or someone above (my apologies if I have . . .), please reply to this email with what you've been working on and the progress made. In addition to the above successes, there is a mountain of background work taking place on many of the other initiatives.

We want to hear from you!

I'd like to ask, to those of you leading pilot projects or just generally involved in these CrewShops- as you make progress on your pilot projects—please let us know of your successes!!. It can be as simple as replying to all on this email!

To ensure you are getting the support you need for your pilots, Marty, Brenda and myself are going to be available most Tuesday›s and Thursday›s in the mezzanine meeting room (now officially rebranded as the "CrewRoom"), from roughly 12:30-1:30. We'd like to hear about the progress you've made on your pilot, or if you just want to kick some ideas around. Of course, if you'd like to reach out to us at other times please do so.

Also posted in the CrewRoom is a Parking Lot board, for any ideas you may have had that we can look at in the near future.

So . . . In closing . . . I'd like to recognize the great efforts that have brought us to this point, and acknowledge that while we do have a ways to go before we create a truly stress free environment able to give our customers exactly what they need when they need it, I'm confident the momentum that has brought us to this point will continue. Intranet site: http://www.ccmscrewshoppilots.com

Thank you, for the early wins, and enjoy your weekend.

Two weeks later Robin received a phone call from Charlie:

Charlie	Robin, I just arrived at work and if I hadn't seen it with my own eyes, I wouldn't have believed it. There's a group of guys from Inbound AND Outbound, walking around our outdoor storage area, reorganizing how we store that stuff to make it easier to turnaround high volume materials—AND NOBODY TOLD THEM TO DO IT!! I don't think I have ever seen anything like it happen here before.
Robin	Just to make sure, is that good or bad?

Charlie   Are you kidding? That's great! That's amazing!
Robin   Cool! What are you going to do to fan it?

Within six weeks the Central Warehouse was turning around all HVM requisitions to the regional stores in one day.

—Pause in the story—

Launching Probes

It is possible and often done, to run an engagement event that concludes with proposals for change that are given to senior management to do with as they see fit. There is nothing wrong with that, but you are now in a planned change scenario, with all the same problems and pressures that change management entails. Imagine if the output of these workshops were a list of ideas that managers took away to discuss and decide what to do with. In my experience, very little would have happened after six weeks, let alone a transformation in actual turnaround.

The reason why generative change produces so much more change more quickly is that people with ideas and motivation are invited to just do it. To those who have not had much experience with generative change, it is always amazing to them how people who are already busy and don't have enough time to do what is already on their plate, will sign up to champion something more and be highly motivated to work on it. But it still helps to launch probes and follow up, in a way that will maximize commitment and momentum.

Launching pilots in a way that engenders commitment needs to take a few things into account. The simple, basic formula for creating commitment in people to act is that they make a 1) voluntary, 2) visible, 3) explicit demonstration of intent. There are many different ways to do this, and how you do it will depend on how many people are involved, the time you have for doing it, cultural norms in the organization, and so on. A basic format is to have people say what they are committing to do without feeling coerced that they have to say anything. If the numbers in the room are too large to do that, you can ask people to write up their commitments and put them on a wall and then have everyone mill about reading these, followed by some publication of the list—perhaps online.

In the case, after the first crewshop, the MT decided they needed to do more to launch the pilots than simply say "go do it" as this was so counter-cultural. They decided that the MT would meet in a separate space, starting about an hour before the crewshop was over. People with a pilot were asked to meet with the MT, explain what they wanted to do, and get some coaching. The explicit message was that the MT was not choosing projects, just coaching, but many people took these meetings as a form of getting permission. That was more important early in the transformation when the idea of employees acting on their ideas was very new. Later its main contribution was to offer sage advice, and sponsorship, from leaders. In either case, this was an effective commitment process and served to amplify the energy to work on the pilot.

The Leader's Role

The role of leadership in a generative change process is very different from traditional planned change but just as critical. The results of successful generative conversations and events will quickly fade if leaders are not paying attention to what is happening, providing timely resources and advice, removing roadblocks, allocating resources, disseminating the learning from success and failures, and celebrating wins.

In typical planned change processes, leaders put most of their effort into the early phases of defining problems and articulating goals and visions. After that, they tend to delegate the actual implementation and focus their attention elsewhere. In some Dialogic OD efforts, a similar thing can happen—all the effort and attention is on designing and organizing the engagement event. But with generative change, the most important time that leaders' attention and effort is needed is after the event. Imagine if leaders had done nothing about those four central pilots that they readily acknowledged could not be successful on their own? A few pilots would have produced some change, but not the transformation in culture (and performance) that the second set of crewshops created. To run successful generative change, it is critical that leaders:

1. Understand that their attention is going to be required to sustain and amplify the momentum that the event generates, and

2. Have access to, and a process for allocating, resources people will need to work on their probes.

One of the things I always do before an event is organize a session where the sponsors and design team brainstorm the kinds of probes that might get generated during the event and then identify what kinds of resources people will need to be successful. Nothing will kill the effort faster than launching probes with groups of people who don't have any allocated time or place to meet.

Table 10 Differences in Leaderships' Role in Planned and Generative Change

Planned Change	Generative Change
Performance-oriented and directive; front-loaded effort.	Possibility oriented and supportive; back-end-loaded effort.
Provide *a vision* of the desired future state.	Name the *purpose* that motivates stakeholders.
Provide resources and clear roles and goals.	Provide resources and clear boundaries.
Provide resources, tools, and techniques that will diagnose the real issues and provide practical solutions.	Provide opportunities to strengthen the relationships and communications that will stimulate the emergence of adaptive actions that people will self-implement.
Accept or reject proposed solutions and direct others to implement.	Encourage self-initiated action. Pay attention to what happens after events and support, scale-up, and embed most promising innovations.
Evaluate outcomes; revise as needed	Disseminate learning; celebrate successes and failures

Tracking and Fanning

Fanning is a key leadership activity in generative change. Fanning is a metaphor based on the image of fanning a small fire into a roaring blaze

(Bushe, 2009). A good Dialogic OD event will start some fires, but you will get much more out of it if you can fan those into bigger changes. Some of the changes will come from pilots and projects, but just as important are the changes in core narratives people hold about "how we do things around here" and the development of a more adaptive organization. You want people to act differently after events because of the increased understanding they have about the nature of their common purpose, the opportunities for improvement that exist, their increased commitment to improving things, and their sense that they have been given license to act on their ideas. All of these are ways in which you are intervening into the social construction of reality, or culture, of the organization, and that needs to be "tracked and fanned" just as much as the pilots.

Before the event, you need to identify and put in place a method for tracking to ensure sponsors know what is happening as a result of the event—not just the pilots, but the more subtle changes in how people are showing up and interacting at work. In the case, this was accomplished by having a "tracker"—a person who was close to the front line, whose role was to pay attention and ensure the sponsors knew what was happening. There are other ways to do this. For example, regular meetings of all the people who were at the crewshop can be organized where people discuss what they are doing, and perhaps identify what they need going forward. These days most people are carrying video recording devices in their phones and can quickly describe and upload to an intranet, a weekly "check-in" on results from the event. What will work in your specific situation with those specific people is up to you, the sponsors, and the design team to work out.

There are many ways to "fan". For example, telling stories about the progress and changes being made to other individuals, at staff meetings, at social events, and so on. The word (through the social network) travels fast. Pretty soon you may hear others telling the same stories. The most important part of fanning is simply noticing, and being seen noticing, whatever it is you want more of. Whatever leaders pay attention to is automatically amplified. Describing what you like and want more of also amplifies. Generic "at-a-boys" are generally not as powerful at amplification as specific, detailed descriptions of the behavior or results that you want to fan. Finding ways to identify and celebrate what was learned from failed pilots will help to fan an innovative, adaptive culture.

Learning from Successes and Failures

One of the pilots that came out of the Outbound Crewshop involved a complete change in how shipments were packed. It required buying new equipment, and the MT had put funds aside so they could do so. The first new pieces of equipment they bought, however, didn't work the way they needed to. Because no one felt responsible for being right, and a tracker was in place, the problem was quickly identified, purchases halted or sent back, and the right equipment was identified and purchased.

It's critical to announce, and act in a way that demonstrates, that people know its OK if their idea or innovation doesn't work, as long as they try and they learn from it. The whole logic of generative change and the use of probes is "learn as you go". In performance-oriented organizations (which businesses have to be), there often develops a culture where it is not OK to fail or make mistakes. That produces a culture that gets in the way of learning, where people hide their failures, work twice as hard on initiatives that won't succeed, spend good money after bad, and justifying doing more instead of regrouping and trying something else. Any move to hold people accountable for probes they initiate will put a damper on people's enthusiasm to propose any future probes and reduce the speed and scope of learning taking place.

Sponsors are often too busy and too distant from the front lines to be aware of all the things that are happening after an engagement event—that's why there needs to be some way of tracking what is taking place and stepping in when it's needed, celebrating wins, and amplifying the momentum. This is especially true of positive changes that don't happen from probes but represent the creation of a more adaptive, agile organization. That needs to be recognized and fanned as well as successful probes. In the case with the team that decided on its own to reorganize the outdoor storage area, the next day Charlie went and found each of them, individually, on the floor. He made sure other people saw him asking them to educate him on what they had learned and done, what if anything they needed from him, and hear him encourage them to do more of it. Of course, news of that spread quickly through the workforce, helping to change the narrative about what was OK for warehouse employees to do. Luckily, in this case, Charlie had seen it happening, but in a lot of cases, senior managers are too busy and distant from the front lines to see these informal, adaptive moves. That's why it is so important to build feedback mechanisms into a generative change process that will not only track the probes but also track how and where there are shifts taking place in the narratives about the organization.

Closing down probes that are failing without leaving a bad taste in people's mouths is a delicate matter. I think it is important to do; otherwise failed probes can become energy black holes. The best way I have seen this happen is for the sponsor to organize a meeting where the problems with the probe are discussed, the lessons from it are identified, and the group who sponsored the probe are asked if they want to continue working on it or put it to rest. If the former, some clear targets are created that identify at what point people agree to let it go. When it is finally put to rest, this is communicated in a celebratory fashion, highlighting what has been learned from it.

Checklist: Before Engagement Events, Prepare to Launch Probes

Here is a checklist of questions that sponsors and design committees ought to have answers for before the engagement event (Roehrig, Schwendenweim & Bushe, 2015):

- ✓ What do we need to do to ensure people believe they really can act differently when they go back to work after the event?
- ✓ Should we do any screening of proposals before people act on them? If so, what screening criteria should we use and how will we do that rapidly and in a way that increases energy and momentum rather than turning people off?
- ✓ What kind of commitment amplifying process will we use at the end of the event?
- ✓ How will we create the time and space for people with busy lives and jobs to take on substantial change initiatives that haven't been defined or budgeted for?
- ✓ What resources and infrastructure are people and groups who are pursuing probes likely to need? How will they get these resources?

- ✓ How do we ensure sponsors know what is happening in a timely way?
- ✓ How can we ensure that barriers and impediments to good ideas are recognized and dealt with?
- ✓ How will we make decisions about what changes to support and resource (or not) and how will we describe this decision-making process and communicate those decisions?
- ✓ How will we spread great new ideas out into the larger organization in a way that will tap into natural networks of allies and supporters, and bring those people into greater engagement during the piloting process?
- ✓ How do we decide that a probe has failed and how will we bring it to an end in a way that sustains people's willingness to propose future probes?

FIVE

Scale Up and Embed Successful Probes

As the change process unfolded at CCMS, Robin focused on designing a few more crewshops to address new issues that emerged, while the managers at CCMS did the important work of tracking and fanning the probes that had emerged from previous crewshops. After ten months of consulting with the team, Robin exited, as they were no longer dependent on him and were able to run generative change processes on their own. In this chapter, we will look at how one of the early probes was amplified by one of the managers into a very significant transformation of Central and Regional warehouse operations without Robin's participation.

The Case

Brenda Swant was wondering what to do next. She had left one of the senior roles on the Management Team to work on the roll-out of an enterprise-wide redesign of all the information technology at Consolidated Construction (an ERP), but the program was a couple of years behind schedule, and she'd been sent back to Material Supply. Her position in CCMS had been filled, and Charlie thought that there was lots she could do helping CCMS get ready for the ERP implementation. Central Warehouse was mostly a paper and pencil operation with desktop computers, far behind best practice in the industry. The MT was well aware that warehouse operations like Amazon were light years ahead in their use of mobile IT technology to digitize receiving and shipping, but they faced many constraints in adopting newer practices. Any software or hardware used at CCMS had to be vetted and approved by a headquarters technology group that was cautious and assertive. Purchasing had to go through many hoops. With the impending ERP system, any improvements had to stay within the current IT system. Plus, they had a fairly disengaged workforce used to the manual systems. There wasn't any training budget nor any budget to purchase equipment. It was tempting to let things slide until the ERP system was already designed and being implemented. Brenda and Charlie, however, felt it would be a mistake to wait too long to figure out how to design and configure the ERP to best meet the needs of CCMS, and to prepare CCMS for it. There were so many things to be done. It was a little difficult to figure out where to start.

As the tracker, she attended the crewshops. During the Inbound HMV turnaround crewshop, one of the pilots gave her an opening. Currently, when a shipment of materials arrived, the receiving crew would make notes of what they had received, and these would pile up on a desk until someone at a desktop entered them into the database. One pilot emerged when a receiver suggested they put a laptop on a movable cart at the docks so the information could be entered immediately when materials arrived. Brenda noticed the small group that proposed this pilot was composed of three 20-somethings interested in technology. Brenda had been given one of the new, company-approved tablets that field supervisors in construction were using. These had been designed for the military, had strong defenses against hacking and intrusions, could be run over by a truck without breaking, and were very expensive. She had discovered that the tablet could run their inventory software so she took it to the pilot group and suggested they play with it and see if it could be used for anything.

That led to several innovations as the pilot group poked and played and found ways to use the tablet for receiving materials. In the past, there was always some uncertainty about what materials had arrived; now there was instant verification. However, they found it annoying having to type all the information into the tablet, and this is when Brenda introduced them to barcoding. Fortunately, the tablets came with built-in barcode scanners, and she bought printers and templates for the group to experiment with. Over the next few months they tried out and settled on the kinds of barcodes they found most appropriate and useful for different materials. By this point, other people in receiving were asking for their own tablets. Brenda could see there was an opportunity to amplify this into something much bigger, and identified "Easier, More Accurate Work" as the purpose for a generative change process, and put a large banner with those words up in the Central Warehouse. Anyone interested in how to create easier, more accurate work was invited to lunchtime conversations in the crewroom where Brenda described opportunities for digitizing operations. Most of the action, however, was still in receiving. Charlie authorized buying more tablets, and all receivers were now collecting information at "point of use", but some questioned if there was a better way to collect the data as the tablets were heavy and cumbersome. This was when Brenda introduced them to small scanners they could wear on their belts that could read the barcodes and transmit the data wirelessly. They were an instant hit. The experimentation expanded from simply receiving, to putting away materials on shelves. Now, not only was it instantly clear what had been received, but also immediately clear when HV materials were on the shelves.

The many benefits from much-increased accuracy and much-increased certainty led Brenda to suggest to Charlie that they barcode the entire warehouse. That would require a massive investment, and there were still many questions about how best to do it. They invited the informal leader of the original pilot group, John, to go on a special project and barcode one aisle in the warehouse. That became his full-time job. There were close to a thousand different catalogs items in this one aisle, and it took John three months, full time, to complete it. During this time, John came up with numerous suggestions for how to better organize the racks to allow for digital transformation, as well as suggestions for what kind of labeling to use.

As John was working on this experiment in barcoding, Brenda was paving the way for greater application of technology. One of the greatest barriers she faced was a negative narrative in the rest of Consolidated Construction toward "mobility". A few years previously, in another part of Consolidated, a very large, very expensive, planned change process to implement mobile practices had failed. That resulted in a corporate narrative that "mobility costs too much for cool gadgets with little payback." Brenda knew that asking for money to support her mobility efforts would get no traction, so she and Charlie invented a different label, "point of use". Charlie began describing the results of the "point of use" trials to senior managers. Brenda used her iPhone to make short videos of warehouse workers describing the benefits of point of use technology that Charlies showed others. They organized plant tours with executives and members of the corporate technology department to witness the changes taking place. At a company town hall meeting with the top 100 managers, Charlie got Brenda on the agenda, and she brought along the pilot team who described how they previously worked, and the big improvements in accuracy and efficiency they were creating from point of use. The corporate Organizational Effectiveness team questioned her change management process—where were her Gant charts, and so on? She responded, "look, there is just me, and I don't have a budget for any of this." The result of Charlie's sponsorship work, managing "the politics", was that applications for capital funding for point of use technology got quickly approved.

After John finished barcoding the aisle, the benefits were apparent to everyone, not just Inbound. While the Inbound team found it was more fun to stock that aisle (references to Star Trek were plentiful), the Order and Scheduling group found it made their work easier and more accurate. It was common for the warehouse to experience a "stockout"—when the inventory system said that material was in the warehouse, but it could not be found. That would require manual inspection, and a lot of detective work, on the part of office staff, and often under pressure to quickly find or replace the material. But it was no longer a problem for anything in that aisle. Similarly, the Outbound department found it was much easier to find and pick materials in that aisle, and they became interested in how they could adapt the technology for their needs.

At this point, Charlie and Brenda held an all-hands meeting of Order & Scheduling and Central Warehouse, where people were invited to discuss the effects they'd seen from point of use technology. Lots of opinions, mostly positive, were shared. The new narrative that emerged was "*easy and accurate is the way stress-free customer service. Barcodes are the way to accurate, and scanners make it easy.*" Charlie concluded by saying, "well, to get the benefits we are going to have to barcode everything." That would not be a small undertaking. It had taken John 3 months to do one aisle—there were 22 more, plus outdoor storage. Printers and scanners were purchased, and the crewroom reorganized into a barcoding shop. All employees were invited to volunteer, and Charlie approved overtime pay for anyone who pitched in. Lots of people did. Folks from the admin offices as well as from the warehouse floor spent many hours, after work and on weekends, and many innovations emerged. Brenda was surprised at the atmosphere that developed in that room—it was fun! There was a sense of camaraderie, lots of laughter, and dinner was brought in for those who stayed late.

While the barcoding was underway, John was assigned a new role, traveling to the regional warehouses to train them on the new technology. His travels raised lots of questions that led to many innovations. For example, in response to a shopkeeper's questions, Brenda got funding to hire a software firm to create an application that allowed keepers to use the scanners, connected to their company iPhones, to order materials with the touch of a button. That vastly increased the ease and accuracy of material requisitions, and the regional storekeepers bought into the digitization effort.

After the first month of the barcoding project, to amplify the momentum and volunteer effort, Charlie challenged the warehouse: if they completed the barcoding within nine months, he would go in the dunk tank at a local attraction. They completed it in six.

In less than two years after the first pilot to put a laptop on a cart, CCMS went from an essentially paper and pencil operation to a fully mobile digital operation. They did it without a vision, without a plan, without external consultants or training, and without much of any "resistance to change". They did it through an emergent, generative change process.

—End of Story—

Leading Generative Change: From Small Flames to Roaring Fires

Anyone who has spent time in organizations has seen how difficult it can be to accomplish what CCMS did (undergo a complete digital transformation) using the standard change management approach. Consolidated had, itself, experienced an earlier failed attempt, leaving leaders in the organization skeptical about the benefits of mobile technology. It is examples like this that lead proponents of generative change processes to declare that they produce more change, more rapidly than conventional planned change. By building on small wins, encouraging an attitude of experimentation and learning as you go, small changes can build up into significant organizational transformations, and in the process, create a more adaptive organization.

However, it requires leadership. In a generative change process, this is where leadership is most critical—AFTER the "events", not before. Generative change requires leaders to work with initial small wins, building on that to accelerate the quantity and quality of innovations that come from the people who will have to make them work, in pursuit of the purpose.

There are many kinds of leadership, and leadership comes from many different places during a generative change process, but here we will focus on three. These are the kinds of leadership exemplified in this chapter by Charlie, Brenda, and John. Inspired by a set of distinctions created by Darryl Connor (1992), I will refer to these as sponsors (Charlie), change agents (Brenda) and stakeholders (John). Table 11 summarizes the following points.

Sponsors are the people who have the authority to mandate change. Typically, they control the money and they can change roles, processes, and procedures. But they have only so much time to attend to anything, so they need change agents who can work full time on specific change efforts. However, the people who will have to change, and will have to be the ones to identify the changes and act on them, are the stakeholders. Let's look at the key roles each of them plays.

Change Agents

Typically, change agents are Dialogic OD practitioners. They can be internal managers or professional staff or external consultants. It's also not unusual to have internal change agents be coached by external consultants. Good change agents are people who can comfortably interact at all levels of the corporate hierarchy. They have to be people to whom stakeholders are willing to tell the truth. Sometimes sponsors are too intimidating—the more distance in the hierarchy, the harder it can be for sponsors to get the unvarnished truth. So it's essential that they get this from their change agents. This means the sponsor—change agent relationship has to be different from the typical senior manager—project leader relationship where the project manager reports to a leader who gives them marching orders. That needs to get turned on its head. It's more the case that the change agent will give the sponsor marching orders—identify where the sponsor needs to show up, who they need to talk to, what message needs to be delivered, and so on. Brenda and Charlie had exactly that kind of relationship, and he acted on all her suggestions and advice.

In a generative change process, change agents work with the flow—they work with the energy and momentum already in the system. Brenda needed to find a way to get CCMS ready for digitization—so she worked with the stakeholders who showed an interest. She tracked what they were doing and at the appropriate moments brought new ideas and opportunities to them. She made sure they got the credit for the changes they created—highlighting them through the videos and presentations to senior leaders. She created a generative purpose: making work easier and accurate, and hosted generative conversations. Notice that these weren't "events" like crewshops. They were much more informal, and that is entirely appropriate. A generative conversation is one where new ideas are generated that people want to act on, and those can be created at any moment, as well as at "events". She found ways to bring others who weren't initially interested into further generative conversations, building on what they cared about to spread the change process.

Stakeholders

Stakeholders provide leadership when they identify and own the changes they want to make. John, a unionized employee at CCMS, is a perfect example of this kind of leadership. He fully engaged with the purpose, because it was inherently motivating to him. Brenda and Charlie found expanded opportunities for him to bring that leadership, first, barcoding the first aisle, and then dispersing the innovations to the regional warehouses. He and his colleagues made and owned the changes they introduced. They communicated and engaged their peers in their ideas, identified what worked and what did not, and created the change. John and others received credit for the changes. They were the ones who made presentations to the senior managers who came on the plant tours: in the videos of the innovations and the senior management town halls. Many stakeholders engaged in the barcoding effort; their acts of voluntary engagement were acts of leadership.

Table 11: Three Leadership Roles in Generative Change

	Sponsor	Stakeholder	Change Agent
Ownership	Supports change Shares ownership	Makes change Owns changes	Champions change Accepts ownership
Identifying the purpose	Identifies the adaptive challenge s/he will put energy into	Engages with the generative image	Helps to reframe the adaptive challenge into a generative image
Mobilizing Engagement	Explains purpose Invites engagement	Informs others Considers engagement	Networks with others Makes the case for engagement
Dialoguing	Sponsors new conversations Creates a safe space for differences	Participates in new conversations Speaks up and listens	Designs and facilitates new conversations Works with the energy
Innovating	Blesses probes Protects from upper level conflicts	Proposes probes Manages day-to-day conflicts	Tracks probes Facilitates learning from conflicts
Improvising	Provides resources for change initiatives Amplifies successes, acknowledges learning from failures	Puts effort into change initiatives Reveals successes and failures	Closes the loop between sponsors and stakeholders on change initiatives Distributes learning from successes and failures
Monitoring Progress	Celebrates results; shares credit	Achieves results; earns credit	Measures results; receives credit
Changing Systems & Structures	Works to design and align systems and structures	Implements new systems and structures	Ensures learning loops are in place

Sponsors

Sponsors provide the environment in which change agents and stakeholders can flourish. Charlie recognized the importance of transforming the use of digital mobility in the warehouse and supported everything Brenda wanted to do. He authorized the purchase of equipment. He authorized John's special assignments. He invited all the stakeholders to participate in the barcoding effort and authorized overtime pay and dinners for them. He consistently created a safe space for people to speak out and to try things that didn't work. He gave credit and celebrated success, happily going into the dunk tank when the organization beat everyone's expectations for completing the barcoding project.

Sponsors also have to manage the dynamics taking place in the rest of the organization. No change happens in a vacuum. Sponsors need to integrate the changes they are sponsoring with other changes taking place in the organization. They have to manage the political dynamics and the narratives that emerge around the change project. We saw how Charlie worked around the negative narrative about mobile technology in the larger corporation so it would not impede what they were trying to achieve. He orchestrated several opportunities to build a positive impression among powerful stakeholders which made it possible to get the resources they needed to be successful. He found ways to realign systems and processes to work with the new digital technology.

Checklist for Scaling Up and Embedding Successful Probes

- ✓ Pay particular attention to probes that are aligned with the big picture, the longer-term desired changes the organization needs.
- ✓ Find ways to work with the willing and build on small wins.
- ✓ Ensure there is a process for leaders to be talking about the structures and processes needed to sustain new practices as they emerge.
- ✓ Organize presentations from teams that have developed probes so they can share their results with relevant stakeholders and identify lessons learned.

- ✓ Ensure there are opportunities for the leadership team to review if and how the current strategy and culture "fits" with newly discovered opportunities.
- ✓ Identify helping and hindering narratives and work at creating new narratives that will support the desired changes.
- ✓ Find opportunities to engage non-engaged stakeholders by identifying and promoting ways in which their wants and concerns can be addressed by the changes, and ways in which they can create probes aligned with both.

Conclusion

Dialogic OD and Generative Change are not synonymous. You can use Dialogic OD for other things, like developing agreement on principles, developing a consensus amongst different stakeholders, working through a conflict between individuals or groups, reducing dysfunctional behaviors, changing how people think and the shared narratives that guide that thinking. These are just some common examples of outcomes OD consultants might work on where a generative change process might not apply.

What is specific and unique about the generative change model is that the focus of generative conversations are to launch probes, and that change comes from engaging those who will have to change in self-initiated actions that are then learned from and built on. Hosting such generative conversations is made easier by using a generative image that attracts the right people into those conversations. Leaders need to bring most of their effort to the backend of the process, ensuring that the energy and ideas that come from events are sustained, used to learn from, and amplified into significant improvements.

In this case, we can see the three core change processes of Dialogic OD, emergence, narrative, and generativity, all at work. Two generative images, "stress free customer service", and "easier, more accurate work", were successful in attracting the right people into useful conversations and actions. The crewshops were designed so that people with similar interests and motivations could find each other, and generate new ideas they wanted to act on. The generative change model is an emergent change process where the endpoint is not known at the start. Perhaps the most significant changes, as they are what leads to lasting change, were changes in the core narratives people held about leadership, change, and CCMS. All the members of the MT went through a significant change in their beliefs about leadership and took those changes with them into significant new jobs. They now see themselves as problem-setters, not problem-solvers. They all embraced a way of leading through conversations that generate emergent solutions. CCMS employees changed their beliefs about their leaders, the organization and themselves. New narratives emerged that supported a culture of engagement where most front line employees now believe they are valued partners in developing new solutions to whatever problems show up. It is now a few years later, and managers from other parts of Consolidated Construction still talk about how different it is to be in a meeting at CCMS, how engaged unionized employees are in managing the work, and how much easier it is to make change happen. And Robin is working once again with Charlie, who got promoted to another part of the organization with a different set of challenges.

Some Non-Issues that Could Be Issues

Things went pretty smoothly in this case. It isn't always that way. Let's look at some of the common problems an OD consultant can run into, that you want to be ready for.

Leaders don't see the value in engagement

In this case, Charlie was a strong advocate, and the rest of the team quickly adopted this perspective after the first few crewshops, but sometimes a key sponsor is not. Common reasons to not hold a crewshop type of event include it will cost too much, it will distract people from their jobs, fear of loss of their own power, perceived lack of knowledge of strategy and context down below, risk of unleashing self-oriented behaviors, fear of loss of control and not "knowing everything" about what is taking place in their department. Your job is to help them see why using a generative approach will solve their problems. Some reasons include deeper ownership, more relevant solutions, improved engagement, observing and providing transparency to lower level key contributors, building an adaptive organization. It can help to have examples of other places that have used generative change processes effectively which you can find online, in magazines like Harvard Business Review and in Bushe & Nagaishi (2018) along with this book. My fervent hope is that the generative change model will help managers better understand what Dialogic OD consultants have been doing successfully for decades.

Contracting for emergent change

When you don't have a client like Charlie, one of the most difficult stages can be getting started when you can't be clear about what, exactly, will happen. Clients expect consultants to map out a sequence of activities toward a clear endpoint, like in change management. Tova Averbuch (2015) has a brilliant chapter on handling entry and contracting for Dialogic OD. Her advice is to begin with a short contract to explore the relevance of a generative change approach, and then use a dialogic OD method with the team that will decide if you are the person to hire. Have them experience a generative approach as they are working on whether a dialogic approach best fits their situation. If they buy-in, then you can contract for the steps in the generative change model.

It's not safe to talk

Though CCMS was a low engagement operation at the beginning, it was not a dangerous one. When Robin entered the MT, he found a group that was comfortable speaking their minds to each other. When people from the field and shop floor came to crewshops, not a lot of time needed to be spent creating a sense that it was safe to speak out. But that is not always the case. Sometimes a change process begins with building the team that will lead it, working first on creating trust and respect amongst the members of the leadership team. Then, when holding engagement events, time might need to be taken, or structures put in place, for trust to build. There are many other books on this topic, and any competent Dialogic OD practitioner should have competence in noticing when safety is an issue and have ideas for how to address that. Making attendance at events voluntary greatly reduces the need to build a safe container.

Managers don't know how to coach

It only took a little coaching from Robin, and the example of Charlie, for the other MT managers to do a good job of showing up as coaches during the crewshops. They knew how to make suggestions without them sounding like commands. They knew how to support the timid into being brave, and how to put up guardrails for the overzealous without losing their energy. But not everyone does. A manager doing a poor job of showing up as a coach during the stage of launching probes can drain energy out of the change effort. As the OD practitioner, you may want to ensure that managers have coaching skills before running engagement events.

Key external stakeholders won't play

In this case, the client was able to make significant changes internally without having to include stakeholders outside of the sponsor's authority. Over time, CCMS did reach out to their users and ran crewshops with, for example, construction crews and shopkeepers. But to do so, they had to line up sponsorship in those other groups first. The first proposal to work with a group outside CCMS involved problem areas with managing vendors, and one CCMS manager was eager to get the different groups in the room and crewshop the problems. Robin, however, insisted they hold back and think through the variety of probes that might emerge and who would have to support them. That led Charlie to have a clarifying conversation with his peer with authority over that other part of the organization, and it became clear that person was not ready to support a generative change process. So the effort was called off. I refuse to run engagement events unless I feel certain the necessary sponsorship exists because I know people will come out of those events charged up. If they then run into a brick wall it creates more cynicism and disillusionment—and the organization is worse off than if nothing had happened.

Systemic blowback

If you significantly change one part of a system, it usually requires changes in other parts of the system. Early in my career, I was involved in some change projects where major improvement at the front lines of organizations led to increasing pressures for more senior leaders to change their behaviors as well. When they didn't, the change process fell apart. That didn't happen at Consolidated Construction, mainly I think, because Material Supply operated fairly independently from the rest of the organization. But in other cases, it's important to be aware that this may happen and plan early for how to engage those other parts of the organization productively. For example, when working in a unionized organization like CCMS it is very important to make sure the union will be OK with the change process as they can quickly derail anything you do. In this case, Charlie had a good relationship with the union stewards in CCMS, and they liked the changes, so there wasn't any blowback from the union. If there is a strained or distrustful relationship, work may have to be done to get the union onside before running events like crewshops.

Closing Comments

I hope you have found the CCMS story inspiring, and my commentary of theories and models helpful, in imagining how you can run a generative change process. After 40 years as an OD practitioner, I have found it the most satisfying change work I do because 1) it fits so well with the OD values of engagement in inquiry, free and informed choice, and development of both the people and the system, and 2) because of how quickly it works to produce more change, more quickly, than anyone expected was possible.

APPENDIX

Robin's meeting notes from the First MT meeting

Robin's notes from Materials Supply Meeting, October 22, 20XX
Present: Charlie, Ester, Marty, Wally, Robin

In response to my probes about "why are we here" the group focused in on the inability of MS to self-regulate the flow of materials. I got the impression they would like to manage the operation like a well-oiled machine but the complexity and variability of the demands made on them make that difficult.

When I questioned whether the situation was too complex and variable for simple standardized solutions, it became clear they believe a lot more standardization (planning) is possible, and would like to focus on that.

There is a belief that the lack of standardized operations is a source of pain for employees and is leading to increased disengagement. Success = did we avoid pain today. While the quality of people is good, lack of clarity about who is responsible for what, what the service level expectations are, unexpected changing expectations and rules, a sense that things get started that don't get finished and a lack of clarity about how does what I do contribute, are all sources of disengagement.

The expectations from their line organization is to stay within headcount and keep users satisfied. This struck me as giving them a fair degree of autonomy and latitude for deciding how best to organize themselves.

Some other things that were said that struck me as important to dig into at some point:

- We don't talk directly to our customers
- We aren't sure if we are a service organization or a supply chain organization
- When we say no to our users, it gets escalated

They believe that they are able to talk straight with each other and sort things out within the management team, but that the structure isolates different groups in Material Supply so that there isn't that kind of communication or coordination lower down.

Our attention focused what makes it difficult to buffer the operating core from uncertainty.

Sources of variability I noted:

External
- Recent XX study laid out a model that was only partially implemented, leading to areas of uncertainty about who is responsible for what.
- Outside units make purchasing decisions and sign up vendors on large, non-standardized items
- Items arrive for warehousing in different sizes and at unpredictable times
- Lack of clarity of the role of MS in purchasing strategy
- Lack of clarity of the role of MS in managing some vendor contracts
- Users saying they want something by some date, but then needing it at a different date
- Users using multiple points of contact within MS to make demands and get service

Internal
- Field store reconfiguration
- Different employees reacting to different user demands differently
- Some "blame game" goes on internally
- Some lack of clarity about which units have authority/responsibility

- Number of acting managers in the field stores

The question the group thought should guide our work is: **How do we create less volatility and greater clarity/agreement so we can achieve 90% of our work within planned/agreed to guidelines?**

I asked the group to think about how that question could be rephrased in a way that would make it a compelling question to employees, the kind of question that people would be willing to crawl over glass to be in conversation about.

I discussed how change efforts, where leaders decide what the solution is and then get others to do it, only work for technical problems, but that they faced an "adaptive challenge", the solution to which would require changes in perceptions, assumptions and beliefs of the people who would have to make the change. To do that, it only works if leaders guide the process of change but engage those stakeholders who have to make the change in proposing and trying out solutions, and then see what works. There seemed to be some buy in to that but I also sensed some hesitation and acknowledgement that would not be common practice in CCMS.

In looking at the sources of variability they faced, they decided they wanted to start by seeing if they could reduce some of the internal variability MS creates for itself and focused in on three:

- Different points of contact with the same user
- Who users call and how those calls get managed
- Planners trying to execute and executers trying to plan

We decided that at the next meeting we would identify

1. Who, exactly, would need to change in order to make any such changes work? In other words, which employees need to be involved in proposing solutions?

2. What kinds of change processes would be most likely to succeed given the issues, culture, players and situational opportunities and constraints MS faces?

We agreed to meet again for a half day in the next two weeks.

References

Argyris, C. (1970) *Intervention: Theory and method*. Reading, MA: Addison-Wesley.

Averbuch, T. (2015) Entering, readiness and contracting for dialogic organization development. In G.R. Bushe & R.J. Marshak (eds.) *Dialogic organization development (219-244)*. Oakland, CA: Berrett-Koehler.

Blake, R.R., Shepard, H.A. & Mouton, J.S. (1964) *Managing intergroup conflict in industry*, Houston, TX: Gulf.

Bushe, G.R. (2013) Generative process, generative outcomes: The transformational potential of appreciative inquiry. In Cooperrider, D., Zandee, D., Godwin, L., Avital, M. and Boland, B. (eds.) *Organizational generativity (Volume 4 in Advances in Appreciative Inquiry, 89-113)* London, UK: Emerald.

Bushe, G.R. (2010) Being the container in dialogic OD. *Practicing Social Change*, 1:2, 10-15.

Bushe, G.R. (2009) *Clear leadership: Sustaining real collaboration and partnership at work*. Boston, MA: Davies-Black

Bushe, G.R. (1998) Appreciative inquiry with teams. *Organization Development Journal*, 16:3, 41-50.

Bushe, G.R., & Marshak, R.J. (2014). The dialogic mindset in organization development. *Research in Organizational Change and Development, 22*, 55-97.

Bushe G.R. & Nagaishi, M. (2018) Standing on the past to imagine the future: Organization development is not (just) about change. *Organization Development Journal*, 36:3, 23-36.

Bushe, G.R. & Paranjapey, N. (2015) Comparing the generativity of problem-solving versus appreciative inquiry: A field experiment. *Journal of Applied Behavioral Science*, 51:3, 309-335.

Bushe, G.R., & Storch, J. (2015). Generative image: Sourcing novelty. In G.R. Bushe & R.J. Marshak (eds.) *Dialogic organization development (101-122)*. Oakland, CA: Berrett-Koehler.

Churchman, C.W. (1967). Wicked problems. *Management Science*. 14:4, B141–B146.

Collins J., & Hansen, M.T. (2011). *Great by choice*. NYC: Harper Business.

Conner, D.R. (1992) *Managing at the speed of change*. NYC, NY: Villard.

Corrigan, C. (2015) Hosting and holding containers. In G.R. Bushe & R.J. Marshak (eds.) *Dialogic organization development (291-304)*. Oakland, CA: Berrett-Koehler.

Eaton, M. (2010) Why change programs fail. *Human Resource Management International Digest,* 18:2, 37-42.

Goppelt. J. & Ray K.W. (2015) Dialogic process consulting: Working live. In G.R. Bushe & R.J. Marshak (eds.) *Dialogic organization development (371-390)*. Oakland, CA: Berrett-Koehler.

Hastings, B. & Schwarz, G. (2019) Diagnostic and dialogic organization development: Competitive or collaborative focuses of inquiry? In Guclu Atinc (Ed.), *Proceedings of the Seventy-ninth Annual Meeting of the Academy of Management.* Online ISSN: 2151-6561.

Heifetz, R.A. (1994) *Leadership without easy answers.* Cambridge, MA: Harvard University Press.

Holman, P. (2010) *Engaging emergence.* San Francisco, CA: Berrett-Koehler.

Holman, P., Devane, T. & Cady, S. (2007) *The change handbook.* San Francisco: Berrett-Koehler.

Johnson, B. (1992) *Polarity management.* NYC, NY: HRD Press.

Lippitt, R., Watson, J. & Westly, B. (1958) *The dynamics of planned change.* NYC, NY: Harcourt, Brace and World.

Marshak, R.J. (2020) *Dialogic process consulting: Generative meaning-making in action.* North Vancouver, BC: BMI Books.

Marshak, R.J. and Bushe, G.R. (2018) Planned and generative change in organization development. *OD Practitioner,* 50:4, 9-15.

McKergow, M. & Bailey, H. (2014) *Host: Six new roles of engagement.* London, UK: Solution Books.

Owen, H. (2008). *Wave rider: Leadership for high performance in a self-organizing world.* San Francisco, CA: Berrett-Koehler.

Quinn, R.E. (1988) *Beyond rational management.* San Francisco: Jossey-Bass.

Roehrig, M., Schwendenwein, J., & Bushe, G.R. (2015). Amplifying change: A three-phase approach to model, nurture and embed ideas for change. In G.R. Bushe & R.J. Marshak (eds.) *Dialogic organization development (325-348)*. Oakland, CA: Berrett-Koehler.

Shaw, P. (2002) *Changing conversations in organizations.* NYC, NY: Routledge.

Smith, K.K., & Berg, D.N. (1987) *Paradoxes of group life.* San Francisco, CA: Jossey-Bass.

Snowden, D. J., & Boone, M. E. (2007). A leader's framework for decision making. *Harvard Business Review,* 85:11, 68-76.

Stacey, R. (2010) *Complex responsive processes in organisations.* London, UK: Routledge.

Stacey, R. (2015) Understanding organizations as complex responsive processes of relating. In G.R. Bushe & R.J. Marshak (eds.) *Dialogic organization development (151-175)*. Oakland, CA: Berrett-Koehler.

Storch, J. (2015) Enabling change: The skills of dialogic OD. In G.R. Bushe & R.J. Marshak (eds.) *Dialogic organization development (197-218)*. Oakland, CA: Berrett-Koehler.

Thompson, J. (1967) *Organizations in action*. NYC, NY: McGraw-Hill.

Towers Watson (2013). Towers Watson change and communication ROI survey. Retrieved from https://www.towerswatson.com/en/Press/2013/08/Only-One-Quarter-of-Employers-Are-Sustaining-Gains-From-Change-Management

Weisbord, M. & Janoff, S. (2007) *Don't just do something stand there! Ten principles for leading meetings that matter*. San Francisco, CA: Berret-Koehler.

Zubizarreta, R. (2014) *From conflict to creative collaboration: A user's guide to dynamic facilitation*. Minneapolis, MN: Two Harbors Press.

BMI Series in Dialogic OD

The BMI series in Dialogic OD, inspired by the original Addison-Wesley Series in OD, is a series of short, 100 page volumes written by experienced Dialogic OD practitioners. Edited by Gervase Bushe and Bob Marshak, each narrowly focuses on one specific aspect of Dialogic OD practice and provides consultants with tested, practical models and processes, along with case examples to make the models come alive.

Dialogic Process Consulting: Generative Meaning-Making in Action

https://b-m-institute.com/books/dialogic-process-consulting/

Robert Marshak introduces a subtle but powerful dialogic OD method that coaches and consultants can use to help clients address limiting assumptions and create new possibilities. The phrase "generative meaning-making in action" captures the essence of the approach. You will learn how to identify and address out-of-awareness mindsets during everyday conversations, how to deeply listen for the implicit mindsets that influence meaning-making in individuals, groups and organizations, and how to intervene through transforming talk to challenge or change them.

The Dynamics of Generative Change

https://b-m-institute.com/books/the-dynamics-of-generative-change/

Gervase Bushe steps you through the Generative Change Model, a way to approach organizational change more aligned with today's needs for an agile and engaged workforce than planned change methods. We follow the case of Consolidated Construction Materials Supply, 200 poorly engaged employees inside a large, traditional construction company. Organized into three fragmented units, this low-tech warehouse and distribution operation transformed into a highly engaged, collaborative, agile and fully digitized one in a little more than two years after the first phone call between the consultant and the Director. They accomplished this without a vision, without a plan, without training, any resistance to change, and only 1 external OD consultant. The book provides advice on the key issues in leading an emergent, generative change process.

Hosting Generative Change: Creating Containers for Creativity and Commitment

http://b-m-institute.com/books/hosting-generative-change/

When the future is uncertain and the past is contested, good hosting can bring hope and co-operation into the present. Any Dialogic OD practice will bring people together for creative conversations, expanded horizons, mutual connection and committed action. The way these events are hosted can make all the difference. **Mark McKergow** brings over a decade of research into the etiquette of hosting in different cultures and eras and combines it with three decades of practice in organizational development and change. The book offers an image of superb hosting as a mix of detailed planning and openness to whatever emerges, taking the lead when needed, with the intent of stepping back as quickly as possible so participants can lead themselves. The book offers a framework of six hosting roles to help navigate the inevitable ups and downs of working with large (and small) groups.

The Team Discovered: Dialogic Team Coaching

http://b-m-institute.com/books/the-team-discovered/

This hopeful, poignant, and deeply insightful book brings the wisdom of Dialogic OD and the heritage of Diagnostic OD into an expansive view of how to best support teams in a world of immense diversity and attention poverty. **Bennett Bratt** offers a new approach to team development that meets today's teams where they live: in a complex world with intense demands and precious little time. This book challenges widely used approaches to team development that utilize data showing a gap between current and desirable team performance. Most methods presume some kind of evaluative comparison is helpful: comparison to other groups, comparison to large data sets, comparison to best practices, comparison to a theoretical ideal. Instead, Ben explains why a dialogic approach to the use of questionnaire data is better at helping teams author their own narrative of effectiveness, one they will own and live into. While showing how to make data useful, Bratt persuasively argues that comparison is at best, a distraction and at worst, debilitating. The book illustrates how to bring the mindsets and tools of Dialogic OD to team coaching through an extended case example.

Future Planned Volumes

From Physical Place to Virtual Space
Gwen Stirling Wilkie

Entry and Contracting for Dialogic OD
Tova Averbuch

Co-Creating the Design Team for Generative Change
Sarah Lewis

If you have an idea for a short (under 30,000 words) book on a specific aspect of Dialogic OD practice, please contact either Gervase (**bushe@sfu.ca**) or Bob (**bobmarshak@aol.com**) to discuss.

Printed in Great Britain
by Amazon